Live Well
Eat Well

Ron
Chicago.

Naturally Peninsula
Tea Flavours

NP

Naturally Peninsula
Tea Flavours

Foreword

Whenever we travel overseas or spend quality time at home in Hong Kong, we always look forward to dim sum or a meal with family and friends. This culinary tradition is summed up in the simple Cantonese expression "yum cha," which means, literally, "drink tea." Such gatherings, unique in their own ways, have been an integral part of life for many different cultures across innumerable generations. For us, the key to the sustainability of this special tradition is tea.

From black tea and oolong tea to green tea, we love the great light taste of the different types of tea, and enjoy collecting and tasting different varieties available around the world. Furthermore, the health benefits that tea has to offer intrigue us and help bring fulfilment to a healthy lifestyle.

Created by the talented culinary teams of each Peninsula Hotel across the globe, this cookbook offers a varied selection of contemporary Asian and Western dishes, ranging from prawns and sashimi to pastas and desserts. Delightfully and creatively, each recipe includes the element of tea, making them even more appealing.

Like wine, tea comes in a variety of flavours, bouquets and vintages. With *Naturally Peninsula – Tea Flavours*, you will be able to experience for yourself the depth and versatility of tea from preparation to tasting. Nevertheless, whether in Hollywood, Hong Kong or any other part of the world, we are truly "cha chee" (Cantonese for "tea aficionados") and we hope that each recipe will take you on an intriguing culinary journey.

Chow Yun Fat and Jasmine Chow

Introduction

When we dine, our senses come alive. We see colours and shapes on the plate and we draw in rising aromas. Eating the food, we are alerted to vibrant flavours, from the sweet burst of ripe mango to the teasing tingle of hot chillies, or to the salty scent of a slow-brewed soy sauce. As we delight in such scrumptious pleasures, we wake to the setting in which we find ourselves. We take in the decorations on the table, the light in the room, the lyrical music. When all such elements are unified, a sense of well being descends.

We yearn for well being. We are drawn to it. Increasingly, in the twenty-first century, we desire a lifestyle that is healthy and in harmony with our surroundings. In other words, we are cheered by what is natural. And very often, the process begins with what we ingest. Along with awakening to pleasure, we like to know that what we eat nurtures us. In turn, if the food is cultivated carefully, we know that we are helping to preserve our environment. We want to be part of that network of earth, water and air that supports us.

Food that delights us should come from a source that is natural. As often as not, that means something free of harmful chemicals and toxins. It should be created with consideration, from unadulterated seed and stock. Producers should care for the food throughout its life cycle with the attention of an artisan. Wild fish, mushrooms and herbs should come from a clean and protected environment and harvested without damaging any ecological surroundings.

Similarly, in the kitchen, the chef should handle what comes from the field and ocean with infinite care, preserving its natural flavours and health-generating properties. Techniques and methods should preserve the nutrition within.

The Peninsula Hotels hopes to promote this kind of well being. We want to delight, engage and entertain our guests. From the food we serve and the ambience in our dining rooms to each service we provide, we aspire to offer the best of living with ease, comfort and beauty in a natural way.

Peninsula kitchens all over the world use top-quality ingredients and our chefs' goal is to prepare the food in healthy ways. They are careful to keep fats, for example, within reasonable limits and to avoid trans fats in their creations. Peninsula dishes look appealing when presented, sending up aromas that tease the appetite before delivering full flavour.

It is The Peninsula Hotels' mission to use, as much as possible, pristine seafood, organic vegetables, fruit and livestock from sustainable sources. And now, with the introduction of tea to its kitchens, our chefs are turning to a proven, superbly healthy, natural ingredient with an ancient lineage and giving it a contemporary twist.

It is a winning combination we hope you will enjoy.

Olivia Wu
Food Consultant

Introduction to Tea

Second only to water, tea is the world's most widely consumed beverage. From delicate and subtle to robust and bold, tea spans a universe of flavours and scents. Eternally reaching across different cultures, tea has long been served in the teahouses of China and in the ascetic ceremonies of Japan, and been turned into the spiced chais of Russia and the Middle East. A strong tea tradition continues to thrive in the time-honoured taking of English afternoon tea and France has championed the rise of *salons du thé*. While it was the British colonialists who began tea plantations in India, it is now tea that defines an Indian way of life.

Every culture claims tea as its own.

The infusion of the leaves of the tree *Camellia sinensis* has stimulated export, exploration and encounter since its discovery in China 3,000 years ago. Trade routes radiated from China to all over the globe and tea wove itself into the cultural, economic and political history of the world. The Chinese character for tea is pronounced "tay" in the Fujian dialect, the sound adopted by much of Western Europe. In several other dialects around China it is pronounced "cha," which took root in other civilisations as "cha" or "chai."

The refreshing, complex taste of tea found instant followers. Yet the immediate experience of well being that comes after sipping brewed tea made an equally strong impression. Tea was first a drink for the nobility, but was then incorporated into medicine. Pu'er tea from Yunnan province, for example, is frequently used in traditional Chinese medicine (TCM).

In the 20th century the Japanese dedicated modern scientific research to the nutritional and medicinal aspects of tea. They and others found compounds in tea that promoted health, notably, large quantities of polyphenols. They discovered that tea, especially green tea, guarded against heart disease, cancer and diabetes, among other ailments. Continuing research in the West, and now China itself, shows that tea is a strong antioxidant and should feature in any healthy 21st century lifestyle.

That is why it is a natural for the chefs of The Peninsula Hotels to come together to create a collection of tea-inspired recipes. From Beijing to Beverly Hills, The Peninsula chefs have employed tea in its myriad forms and flavours. You will find here, tea of the *Camellia sinensis* variety, as well as pure herbal infusions such as raspberry, lemongrass and mint. They are used dry, steeped, ground or whole, and with other ingredients they contribute to the stunning flavour profiles of every dish, from soups to sweets.

We invite you to compose a complete meal from these recipes. The tea flavours are clean and light, yet subtle and sophisticated. And, of course, they enhance well being.

The Peninsula Hotels

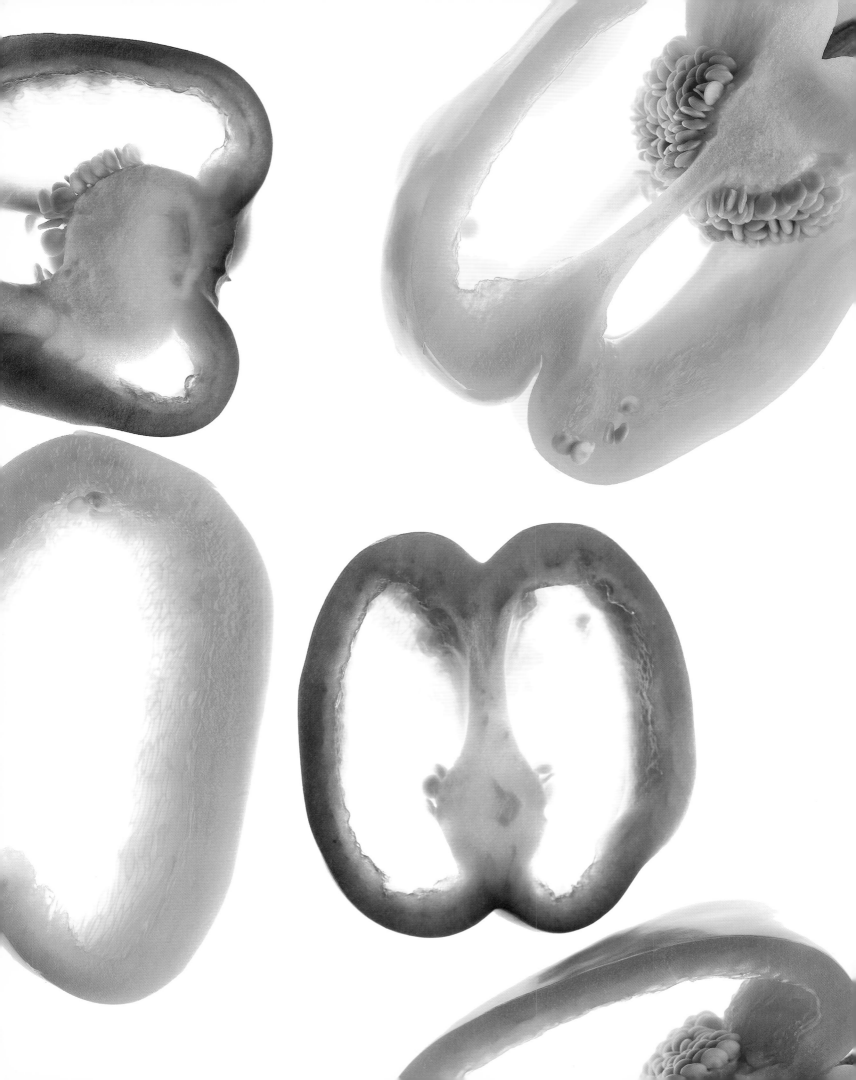

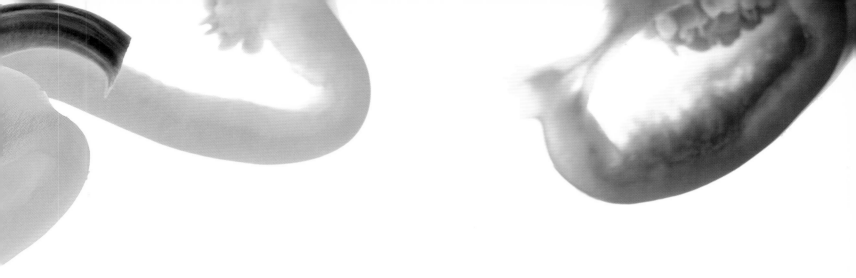

Appetisers

The first course lifts the curtain on any meal and draws attention to the table and the drama to unfold. This prologue should tantalize, enchant, seduce and excite. It piques the appetite. It promises the world.

The following dishes deliver on this promise. They have been created by the chefs of the eight Peninsula properties from the eastern rim of the Pacific to the western rim of the Atlantic. The chefs have scoured the planet for ingredients, cooking techniques and secrets of healthy eating from all cultures. Here you will find Maine lobsters smoked with tea leaves; an Earl Grey-scented wild salmon that relies on Scandinavian gravlax-preparation techniques; and sashimi, which is given a whimsical touch by a crispy strip of pastry. Each declares, "All the world's a stage."

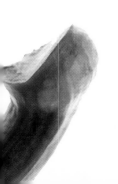

Pan-Seared Scallops with Jasmine Tea and Fuji Apple Fondant

Preparation Time: 2 hours   Cooking Time: 30 minutes   Serves 4

SCALLOPS

Diver scallops *12*

Salt *to taste*

Ground white pepper *to taste*

Unsalted butter or olive oil *for frying*

SAUCE

Garlic *55 g (2 oz), peeled and minced*

Shallots *55 g (2 oz), peeled and minced*

White wine *235 ml (7¹/₂ fl oz)*

Hard cider *475 ml (15 fl oz)*

Fish stock *(see pg 179) 475 ml (15 fl oz)*

Jasmine tea leaves *30 g (1 oz)*

Unsalted butter or margarine *55 g (2 oz), softened*

FUJI APPLE FONDANT

Shallots *55 g (2 oz), peeled and minced*

Garlic *1 clove, peeled and minced*

Fuji apple *1, diced or scooped using a 1-cm (¹/₂-in) melon baller*

APPLE WEDGES (OPTIONAL)

Apple *1*

Sugar or sugar substitute *200 g (7 oz)*

Water *240 ml (8 fl oz / 1 cup)*

GARNISH

Endive leaves

Prepare scallops. Preheat oven to 220°C (440°F). Season scallops with salt and pepper. Heat butter or olive oil in an oven-safe frying pan. Fry scallops until golden on both sides, then place in hot oven to cook for 3 minutes. Remove scallops and keep warm.

Prepare sauce. Sweat garlic and shallots in a pan until tender. Deglaze with wine, scraping bottom of pan. Cook until most of wine evaporates. Add cider, again boiling off most of liquid. Add fish stock and bring to a boil, then add jasmine tea leaves and infuse over low heat for 3 minutes. Strain and discard tea leaves. Reduce remaining liquid to 250 ml (8 fl oz / 1 cup). Whisk in butter or margarine.

Prepare apple fondant. Sweat shallots and garlic in a pan until tender. Add apple and cook until caramelized.

Prepare apple wedges. Preheat oven to 120°C (250°F). Cut apple into small wedges, then smooth edges using a paring knife. Set aside. Place sugar and water in small pot and cook until sugar is dissolved. Add apple wedges and return to a boil. Lower heat and simmer for 1 minute. Remove apple wedges and place on a non-stick silicone baking mat. Place in oven and bake until crisp. Takes about 1 hour. Apple wedges can be prepared at most 4 hours in advance. Store in a dry place until ready to serve.

Serve scallops with apple fondant and wedges. Drizzle with sauce and garnish with endive leaves.

Earl Grey Tea-Cured Salmon with Fennel and Blood Orange Salad

Start preparations 1 day ahead   Cooking Time: 1 hour   Serves 4

SALMON

Wild king salmon *240 g (8¹/₂ oz)*

Earl Grey tea leaves *20 g (²/₃ oz)*

Kosher salt *225 g (8 oz)*

Sugar *140 g (5 oz)*

FENNEL AND BLOOD ORANGE SALAD

Olive oil *2 Tbsp*

Fennel bulb (see Glossary) *316 g (11¹/₂ oz), cut into 0.5-cm (¹/₄-in) cubes*

Salt or salt substitute *to taste*

Freshly cracked black pepper *to taste*

Blood orange *1, peeled and segmented*

SALMON SKIN CRISP

Salmon skin *1 piece*

Light soy sauce *250 ml (8 fl oz / 1 cup)*

Sake *250 ml (8 fl oz / 1 cup)*

ROCKET PURÉE

Rocket leaves *10 g (¹/₃ oz)*

GARNISH (OPTIONAL)

Micro rocket

Finely sliced fennel bulb

Salmon roe

Prepare salmon. Scale salmon and fillet skin. Set skin aside for salmon skin crisp.

Prepare curing mix for salmon. Place tea leaves in a dry sauté pan over medium heat for 30 seconds to release its aroma. Remove tea leaves from pan and leave to cool before blending to a powder in a spice grinder or small, clean electric coffee grinder (see Kitchen Techniques). Mix well with salt and sugar.

Sprinkle curing mix on both sides of salmon. Cover and refrigerate for 6 hours, then turn salmon over and refrigerate for another 6 hours or overnight. Rinse salmon and pat dry with a paper towel. Cover salmon with plastic wrap and keep refrigerated until ready to serve.

Prepare fennel and blood orange salad. Heat a sauté pan over medium high heat and add 1 Tbsp olive oil. Add diced fennel and cook for 5 minutes, or until caramelized. Season to taste with salt and pepper. Remove from heat and toss with blood orange segments and remaining olive oil.

Prepare salmon skin crisp. Scrape layer of fat from skin and rinse thoroughly for 15 minutes under cold running water. Dry skin, then marinate in soy sauce and sake for 30 minutes. Remove skin from marinade and pat dry. Place skin between 2 sheets of greaseproof paper and bake at 180°C (350°F) for 30 minutes. Cut into shape while skin is hot. Leave to cool and harden.

Prepare rocket purée. Blanch rocket in boiling water for 10 seconds. Drain and plunge into iced water, then drain and purée in a blender.

Slice prepared salmon into portions about 60 g (2 oz) each and serve with fennel orange salad. Garnish with salmon skin, micro rocket, finely sliced fennel and salmon roe. Drizzle with rocket purée.

Orange Pekoe Tea-Smoked Lobster with Mango and Cucumber Salad

Preparation Time: 45 minutes   Cooking Time: 25 minutes   Serves 4

SMOKED LOBSTER

Maine lobsters *2, each about 680 g (1¹/₂ lb)*

Orange pekoe tea leaves *475 g (1 lb 1 oz)*

White rice *475 g (1 lb 1 oz)*

Brown sugar *475 g (1 lb 1 oz)*

SALAD

Cucumbers *2*

Ripe mangoes *2, peeled*

Yam bean (jicama) *115 g (4 oz)*

Radish *1 bulb*

Endive *1 head*

Frisée (see Glossary) *1 head*

DRESSING

Vanilla bean *1*

Honey or sugar substitute *28 g (1 oz)*

White wine *235 ml (7¹/₂ fl oz)*

Water *235 ml (7¹/₂ fl oz)*

Olive oil *2 Tbsp*

Rice wine vinegar *60 ml (2 fl oz / 4 Tbsp)*

Salt or salt substitute *to taste*

Ground white pepper *to taste*

GARNISH

Daikon sprouts

Prepare to smoke lobsters. Bring a pot of water to a boil and add a pinch of salt. Blanch lobsters for 4 minutes. Remove lobster meat from shell and smoke lobsters for 2 minutes or until cooked (see Kitchen Techniques).

Prepare salad. Thinly slice cucumbers, mango, yam bean and radish. Using a ring cutter similar in size to the circumference of cucumbers, cut out rounds from the slices. Combine ingredients for salad and toss well. Use remaining pieces of mango in dressing.

Prepare dressing. Place mangoes in a pot with vanilla bean, honey or sugar, wine and water. Cook over medium heat until tender. Takes about 2 minutes. Remove vanilla bean and purée remaining mixture in a blender. Whisk in oil and vinegar, then season with salt and pepper to taste.

Serve smoked lobsters with salad. Drizzle with dressing and garnish with daikon sprouts.

Toro Tuna Sashimi with Elderberry Tea Crisps and Avocado Cream

Preparation Time: 30 minutes   Cooking Time: 5 minutes   Serves 4

PASTA DOUGH

Water *200 ml (6¹/₂ fl oz)*

Elderberry tea leaves *30 g (1 oz)*

Plain flour *500 g (1 lb 1¹/₂ oz)*

Eggs *3*

Egg yolk *1*

Salt or salt substitute *1 tsp*

Soy bean oil *2 Tbsp*

Vegetable oil *for deep-frying*

AVOCADO CREAM

Avocado *¹/₂*

Lemon juice *¹/₂ tsp*

SASHIMI

Freshly cracked black pepper *to taste*

Toro tuna *320 g (11²/₃ oz), thinly sliced*

GARNISH

Elderberry tea leaves

Wasabi sprouts

Elderberry tea powder
  (see Kitchen Techniques)

NOTE

In keeping with the quality of the pasta dough, the quantity given for the dough is enough to make four main courses of pasta. This recipe only requires about one-eighth of the portion. You may use the remaining pasta dough for making noodles, if desired.

Prepare pasta. Heat water to 70°C (155°F) and add tea leaves. Cover and steep for 5 minutes, then strain and discard leaves. Allow tea to cool. Combine flour, eggs and egg yolk, tea infusion, salt and oil in a food processor to form dough. Cut out one-eighth of dough and cover well with plastic wrap. Leave refrigerated for 2–4 hours. Use remaining dough for making pasta, if desired. Roll chilled dough out into a sheet about 0.3-cm (1/10-in) thick and cut into thin strips (see Kitchen Techniques). Heat vegetable oil for deep-frying. Deep-fry pasta strips until crisp. Drain well and set aside. You may do this up to 4 hours before serving.

Prepare avocado cream. Dice avocado and purée with lemon juice.

Prepare sashimi. Crack black pepper over tuna and top with avocado cream.

Serve pasta with tuna and avocado cream. Garnish with tea leaves, wasabi sprouts and tea powder.

Roasted Maine Lobster with Matcha and Grilled Asparagus

Preparation Time: 30 minutes   Cooking Time: 20 minutes   Serves 4

LOBSTERS

Maine lobsters *2, each about 500 g (1 lb 1½ oz)*

Ground white pepper *to taste*

Matcha (green tea powder) *½ tsp*

Olive oil *2 Tbsp*

GRILLED ASPARAGUS

Green and white asparagus *20 spears, peeled*

Olive oil *2 Tbsp*

Salt or salt substitute *to taste*

ASPARAGUS PURÉE

Olive oil *2 Tbsp*

Onion *1, peeled and finely chopped*

Green asparagus *4 spears*

White asparagus *4 spears*

GARNISH (OPTIONAL)

Lobster roe powder

Bring a large pot of water to a rolling boil. Remove lobster claws and cook in boiling water for 3 minutes. Remove and plunge into iced water to stop the cooking process. As soon as claws are cool enough to handle, crack shells and remove meat (see Kitchen Techniques). Set aside. Cut each raw tail into 2 even pieces with shell on. Season with salt, pepper, matcha and a drizzle of olive oil. Set aside.

Prepare asparagus. Toss asparagus in olive oil and season with salt and pepper. Place asparagus spears on a preheated grill and cook approximately 4 minutes, turning frequently.

Prepare green and white asparagus purées. Heat half the olive oil in a frying pan and sauté half the onion until soft. Add green asparagus and cook until very tender. Place into a blender with just enough liquid to cover asparagus spears halfway. Purée until smooth, adjust seasoning and strain through a fine strainer. Repeat process with white asparagus. Set aside for serving.

Prepare lobsters. Add remaining olive oil to a hot pan. Add lobster tail sections and sauté for 3 minutes. Add claw meat and cook for another 30 seconds. Season with salt and pepper to taste and remove onto paper towels to drain. Reserve residue at bottom of pan to be used as sauce.

Serve lobsters with grilled asparagus. Drizzle with sauce from the sauté and garnish with lobster foam, lobster roe powder and asparagus purée. Serve immediately.

Silver Needle Jasmine Scallop with Ginger Panna Cotta and Yuzu

Preparation Time: 8–9 hours   Cooking Time: 45 minutes   Serves 4

SCALLOP

Sushi-grade sea scallop *1, about 70 g (2¹/₂ oz)*

Yuzu or lemon juice *to taste*

Fleur de sel *a pinch*

GINGER PANNA COTTA

Soy milk *285 ml (9 fl oz)*

Skimmed milk *285 ml (9 fl oz)*

Ginger *15 g (¹/₂ oz), peeled and sliced*

Salt or salt substitute *a pinch*

Gelatine sheets *3 leaves*

Lemon *1, grated for zest*

Lime *1, grated for zest*

SILVER NEEDLE TEA BROTH

Mirin *115 ml (4 fl oz)*

Sake *115 ml (4 fl oz)*

Light soy sauce *1 Tbsp*

Water *115 ml (4 fl oz)*

Jasmine silver needle tea leaves *a pinch*

GARNISH (OPTIONAL)

Finely diced water chestnuts

Coriander flowers

Silver needle jasmine tea leaves

Finely grated orange zest

Finely grated lime zest

Finely grated red radish

Prepare ginger panna cotta. Place soy milk, skimmed milk, ginger and salt into a saucepan and bring to gentle boil for 5–10 minutes. Soften gelatine sheets in cold water, then drain excess water before adding to hot milk mixture. Stir to dissolve gelatine completely. Stir in lemon and lime zest, then refrigerate until set. Takes at least 8 hours.

When panna cotta is almost ready, prepare rest of the dish. If necessary, remove tough tendon from side of scallop, then slice scallop into 4 rounds, each about 0.3-cm (¹/₁₀-in) thick.

Prepare silver needle tea broth. Place all liquid ingredients in a saucepan and bring to a boil. Remove from heat and add tea leaves. Let steep for 1 minute, then strain immediately. Refrigerate and allow to chill completely.

To serve, drizzle yuzu or lemon juice over scallop slices. Cut panna cotta into 4 square pieces and top with scallop slices. Sprinkle with fleur de sel and drizzle with silver needle tea broth. Garnish with water chestnuts, coriander flowers, tea leaves, orange and lime zest and red radish.

Passion Fruit Tea-Cured Salmon with Vegetable Crisps and Oolong Tea Mousseline

Start preparations at least 6 hours ahead   Cooking Time: 30 minutes   Serves 4

SALMON

Water *125 ml (4 fl oz / 1/2 cup)*

Raspberry tea *1 sachet*

Passion fruit tea *1 sachet*

Fresh skinless and boneless wild salmon fillet *300 g (11 oz)*

Orange *1, sliced with skin on*

Black peppercorns *10 g (1/3 oz)*

Sugar or sugar substitute *75 g (2 1/2 oz)*

Salt or salt substitute *40 g (1 1/2 oz)*

Dill *45 g (1 1/2 oz)*

VEGETABLE CRISPS

Beetroot *60 g (2 oz)*

Carrot *60 g (2 oz)*

Yam (taro) *60 g (2 oz)*

Tomato *60 g (2 oz)*

Potatoes *60 g (2 oz)*

Fennel bulb (see Glossary) *60 g (2 oz)*

Taro root *60 g (2 oz)*

Ginger *60 g (2 oz)*

Canola oil *for deep-frying*

Plain flour *30 g (1 oz)*

Togarashi pepper *1 tsp*

Salt or salt substitute *a pinch*

OOLONG TEA MOUSSELINE

Oolong tea *1 sachet*

Boiling water *1 Tbsp*

Light crème fraîche *45 g (1 1/2 oz)*

Plain fat-free yogurt *45 g (1 1/2 oz)*

Chives *5 g (1/6 oz), finely sliced*

Salt or salt substitute *to taste*

Ground white pepper *to taste*

GARNISH

Mixed fresh herbs (basil, dill, tarragon and parsley)

Elderberry flowers (optional)

Prepare salmon. Bring water to a boil, then remove from heat. Add raspberry and passion fruit tea sachets and leave to steep for 10 minutes. Allow infusion to cool. Place salmon in a glass or ceramic pan. Pour tea infusion over salmon, then add orange slices, peppercorns, sugar, salt and dill. Cover with plastic wrap and refrigerate for at least 6 hours, preferably overnight. Turn salmon over after 3 hours. Remove salmon from liquid and discard seasoning. Refrigerate until ready to slice.

Prepare vegetable crisps. Peel and cut vegetables into very thin slices, ideally using a mandoline. Heat oil to 180°C (350°F). Dust slices with flour and deep-fry until crisp. Drain well on paper towels. Season with togarashi pepper and salt. Crisps can be prepared 8 hours ahead and stored in a dry place.

Prepare mousseline. Steep tea in boiling water for 10 minutes, then remove tea sachet and allow infusion to cool. Combine with crème fraîche and yogurt. Add chives and season with salt and pepper to taste.

Slice salmon thinly, holding the knife at an angle almost parallel to the cutting board.

Layer salmon slices on a plate with tea mousseline in between and serve with vegetable crisps. Garnish with fresh herb sprigs and elderberry flowers. Serve immediately.

Soups

Soups warm the soul, which is why they are among the most civilised dishes with which to open a meal. In many cultures, soups also represent the most health-giving of dishes, containing the essence of the most important compounds in food. Often it is the slow and lengthy cooking of ingredients in liquid that empowers them with complete nutritional properties.

Tea is an extraction of the tea leaf *Camillia sinensis* or of other herbs, so when tea is combined with soup the result is a powerhouse of energy and health. At the same time, as you will find in this chapter, deep and subtle flavours emerge, giving you the kind and satisfaction only soup can offer.

Ginger Chicken Soup with Ceylon Tea

Preparation Time: 30 minutes   Cooking Time: 15 minutes   Serves 4

CHICKEN SOUP

Chicken stock (see pg 178) *750 ml (24 fl oz / 3 cups)*

Ceylon tea leaves *30 g (1 oz)*

Pepper leaves *10 g (1/3 oz)*

Vegetable oil *1 Tbsp*

Shallots *30 g (1 oz), peeled and chopped*

Ginger *30 g (1 oz), peeled and finely minced*

Boneless dark chicken meat *280 g (10 oz), cut into 1.5-cm (1/4-in) cubes*

Salt or salt substitute *to taste*

Ground white pepper *to taste*

Carrot *100 g (3 1/2 oz), peeled and cut into 1-cm (1/2-in) cubes*

Sweet potato *100 g (3 1/2 oz), peeled and cut into 1-cm (1/2-in) cubes*

GARNISH (OPTIONAL)

Purslane leaves or other greens

Prepare chicken soup. Bring one-third of chicken stock to a boil. Remove from heat and add Ceylon tea and pepper leaves. Let steep for 5 minutes, then strain and discard tea and pepper leaves. Set aside.

Heat vegetable oil in a pan over medium heat. Sauté shallots and ginger until shallots are transparent.

Stir in chicken cubes, then season with salt and pepper to taste. Cover with remaining stock and simmer for 5 minutes. Add carrot and sweet potato.

Bring to a boil and simmer until vegetables are tender. Just before serving, add tea mixture. Bring to a simmer and serve immediately. Garnish with purslane leaves or other greens.

Herbal Black Chicken Tea

Preparation Time: 12 hours   Cooking Time: 4 hours   Serves 4

CONSOMMÉ

Black chicken *1, about 400 g (14¹/₃ oz)*

Water *2 litres (64 fl oz / 8 cups)*

Egg whites *3*

Boneless chicken meat *280 g (10 oz), cut into small pieces*

TEA

Black chicken *1, about 400 g (14¹/₃ oz)*

Cordyceps *25 g (1 oz)*

Wild ginseng (see Glossary) *4 g (¹/₈ oz)*

Sea salt *¹/₂ tsp*

Prepare consommé. Rinse chicken thoroughly and place in a stockpot with water. Simmer over low heat for 8 hours. Strain and cool.

To clarify stock, place egg whites and boneless chicken meat in a food processor and purée for 5 minutes, or until smooth.

Pour cooled stock into a pot and whisk in chicken and egg white mixture. Slowly bring stock up to a simmer, stirring constantly, making sure that egg white does not stick to bottom of pot. A crust or "raft" will form on top of the stock. Once simmering, cut a small hole in the centre of the raft and let stock simmer on low. Do not boil, as the raft might break, causing the stock to become cloudy. Any fat and solid impurities in the stock will attach themselves to the egg white, leaving a beautifully transparent consommé. Ladle stock carefully through the hole in the raft and into a strainer lined with cheesecloth. Set aside and allow to cool. Store refrigerated.

Prepare tea. Clean chicken thoroughly and remove skin and fat. Rinse cordyceps and ginseng with cold water. Combine chicken, cordyceps, ginseng, salt and chilled consommé in a deep heatproof bowl and cover with plastic wrap. Place bowl over a double boiler and cook over simmering water for 4 hours. Strain tea and serve hot in individual serving bowls.

Lemongrass-Caramel Tea Broth with Edamame Wontons and Tofu

Preparation Time: 1 hour 30 minutes   Cooking Time: 45 minutes   Serves 4

Firm tofu *420 g (15 oz)*

TOFU MARINADE

Orange *1, juice extracted*

Roughly chopped ginger *2 Tbsp*

Garlic *1 clove, peeled and crushed*

Spring onion *1, chopped*

Light soy sauce *250 ml (8 fl oz / 1 cup)*

Water *60 ml (2 fl oz / 4 Tbsp)*

Rice wine vinegar *60 ml (2 fl oz / 4 Tbsp)*

Mirin *1 Tbsp*

TOFU BROTH

Garlic *1 clove, peeled and crushed*

Shallot *1, peeled and sliced*

Roughly chopped ginger *2 Tbsp*

Lemongrass (see Glossary) *2 stalks, use only bottom half, cut into 2.5-cm (1-in) lengths*

Grapeseed oil *2 Tbsp*

Vegetable stock (see pg 179) *250 ml (8 fl oz / 1 cup)*

Coconut juice *320 ml (10²/₃ fl oz)*

Caramel tea leaves *4 Tbsp*

Coriander leaves *4 sprigs*

EDAMAME WONTONS

Shallot *1, peeled and minced*

Grapeseed oil *1 Tbsp*

Frozen edamame *250 g (9 oz), removed from pods*

Vegetable stock (see pg 179) *2 Tbsp*

Salt or salt substitute *to taste*

Ground white pepper *to taste*

Wonton wrappers *8 sheets*

Egg *1, lightly beaten*

Baby bok choy *4 stalks*

Enoki mushrooms *1 pack, base trimmed*

Red chilli *1, thinly sliced*

Prepare tofu. Cut firm tofu into 4 slices. Combine marinade ingredients, pour over tofu and refrigerate overnight. Just before serving, remove tofu from marinade, pat dry and sear in a non-stick pan until brown on both sides.

Prepare tofu broth. Place garlic, shallot, ginger, lemongrass and oil in a medium saucepan over low heat. Cook until tender, then add vegetable stock and simmer for 20 minutes. Add coconut juice and return to a simmer. Add caramel tea leaves and coriander sprigs and remove from heat. Allow to steep for 3 minutes. Strain and chill.

Prepare filling for wontons. Lightly sweat shallot in grapeseed oil. Add edamame and vegetable stock. Bring to a simmer and remove from heat. Strain solids and reserve liquid. Place solids in a blender and purée, adding just enough stock to lightly thin out purée. Season to taste with salt and pepper. Chill purée.

To make wontons, place 1 tsp chilled purée on a wonton skin. Brush skin with beaten egg and fold skin over into a half-circle. Bring corners together and seal with more beaten egg. Repeat until ingredients are used up. Blanch in salted boiling water for about 10 seconds, then drain.

To serve, reheat prepared broth. In the meantime, blanch bok choy in lightly salted boiling water for about 10 seconds. Remove and plunge immediately into iced water to stop the cooking process. Drain. Place browned tofu, wontons, bok choy and enoki in hot broth. Garnish with red chilli and serve immediately.

Cantaloupe Soup with Peppermint Lobster Salad

Preparation Time: 2 hours   Cooking Time: 20 minutes   Serves 4

Cantaloupe *550 g (1 lb 4 oz), peeled, seeded and diced*

SALAD

Lobster meat (see Kitchen Techniques) *350 g (12 oz), chopped*

Plain non-fat yogurt *60 ml (2 fl oz / 4 Tbsp)*

Minced shallots *2 tsp*

Chopped tarragon *1 tsp*

Peppermint tea infusion *120 ml (4 fl oz / ¹⁄₂ cup)*

GARNISH

Diced honeydew

Mint leaves

Reserve 4 Tbsp diced cantaloupe for garnish. Juice remainder of cantaloupe, then strain through a fine sieve. Add tea infusion and refrigerate to chill for at least 2 hours.

Prepare salad. Combine salad ingredients, adding more yogurt, if necessary, to hold salad together. Pack salad into 4 small moulds and unmould them into the centre of 4 soup bowls. Pour chilled soup into bowls around salad.

Garnish with reserved diced cantaloupe, honeydew and mint leaves and serve immediately.

Ham Broth with Mustard Greens and Dragonwell Tea Infusion

Preparation Time: 10 minutes   Cooking Time: 30 minutes   Serves 4

HAM BROTH

Sliced Chinese ham *50 g (2 oz)*

Chinese mustard greens (see Glossary) *80 g (3 oz)*

Water *190 ml (6¹/₃ fl oz)*

Dragonwell (*Long Jing*) tea leaves *15 g (¹/₂ oz)*

Chicken stock (see pg 178) *190 ml (6¹/₃ fl oz)*

Salt or salt substitute *to taste*

Sugar or sugar substitute *to taste*

GARNISH (OPTIONAL)

Finely sliced spring onion

Ground, toasted pork skin (*chicharrón*)

NOTE
Use a high quality Chinese ham for this dish. If unavailable, use Smithfield ham.

Prepare ham broth. Place ham in a small saucepan and cover with water. Simmer over low heat for 10 minutes. Drain, reserve stock and set ham aside.

Boil mustard greens in reserved ham stock until tender. Drain and immediately cool in iced water. Drain and set aside.

Bring water to a boil and add tea leaves. Cover and steep for 1 minute, then strain and discard leaves.

In a wok, heat chicken stock, reserved ham and mustard greens and simmer until near boiling. Season with salt and sugar to taste. Pour in tea infusion and bring to a near boil. Serve immediately, garnished with sliced spring onion and ground toasted pork skin, if desired.

Fish

Fish contain some of the most delicate proteins handled in the kitchen. Their flavours must be gently preserved and their omega-3 fatty acids, so important to cardiovascular health, must be retained. The delicacy of fish also demands the greatest creativity and the lightest of touches from chefs. The Peninsula chefs have met these demands in the following recipes.

The Peninsula Hotels supports sustainability in the kind of seafood with which we cook. As with our use of organically produced vegetables and grains, we hope to help safeguard global stocks of fish, which are among the last remaining wild foods we consume. By maintaining a diversity of fish in the oceans, we save the oceans. Increasing demand for food for good health brings with it the threat of over-fishing. That is why, wherever possible, we offer species caught by ocean-friendly and eco-friendly means, avoiding the use of fish that are endangered. In this way, we wish to help perpetuate sources of delicious, nourishing wild seafood for ourselves and our children.

Seared Ahi Tuna with Coconut-Braised Fennel and Jasmine Tea Rice

Preparation Time: 30 minutes   Cooking Time: 35 minutes   Serves 4

JASMINE TEA RICE

Water *500 ml (16 fl oz / 2 cups)*

Green jasmine tea leaves *10 g (¹/₃ oz)*

Jasmine rice *250 g (9 oz)*

Salt or salt substitute *1 tsp*

Olive oil *2 Tbsp*

Onion *1, peeled and diced*

White honshimeji mushrooms *110 g (4 oz)*

FENNEL

Olive oil *2 Tbsp*

Fennel bulb (see Glossary) *1, cut into wedges*

Pernod *85 ml (2¹/₂ fl oz / ¹/₃ cup)*

Coconut milk *125 ml (4 fl oz / ¹/₂ cup)*

AHI TUNA

Ahi tuna steaks *4, each about 110 g (4 oz)*

Salt or salt substitute *to taste*

Freshly ground black pepper *to taste*

Jasmine tea powder *to taste*

Ground pink peppercorns (see Glossary) *to taste*

Prepare jasmine tea rice. Bring water to a boil with green jasmine tea leaves for 2–3 minutes. Strain and combine tea infusion with rice and salt. Return to a boil, then turn heat to low. Cover pan and simmer for 20 minutes.

In a frying pan over medium heat, add olive oil and sauté onion, then add mushrooms and sauté until soft. Stir mixture gently into cooked rice.

Prepare fennel. In a separate frying pan, heat olive oil and sauté fennel wedges until slightly caramelized. Takes about 5 minutes. Remove fennel. Pour Pernod into pan and cook until alcohol is evaporated. Alternately ignite liquid, keeping it safely away from you. Pour in coconut milk and bring to a boil. Return fennel to pan and cook over medium heat.

Prepare ahi tuna. Sprinkle tuna steaks with salt and pepper to taste, then sear in a hot pan for 30–45 seconds per side. The centres should be rare. Remove and dust with tea powder and ground pink peppercorns.

Serve ahi tuna with jasmine tea rice and fennel. Garnish as desired.

Black Tea-Crusted Shimonoseki Sea Bream with Forbidden Black Rice and Citrus Salsa

Start preparations 1 hour before serving   Cooking Time: 15 minutes   Serves 4

CITRUS SALSA

Lemon *1*

Orange *1*

Grapefruit *¹/₂*

Onion *30 g (1 oz), peeled and chopped*

Ginger *15 g (¹/₂ oz), peeled and grated*

Tomatoes *60 g (2 oz), peeled, seeded and diced*

Olive oil *45 ml (1¹/₂ fl oz / 3 Tbsp)*

Coriander leaves *15 g (¹/₂ oz), chopped*

Salt or salt substitute *to taste*

Ground black pepper *to taste*

RICE

Vegetable stock (see pg 179) *1.1 litres (35 fl oz)*

Onion *45 g (1¹/₂ oz), peeled and chopped*

Olive oil *1 Tbsp*

Forbidden black rice *240 g (8¹/₂ oz)*

SEA BREAM

Skinless sea bream fillets *4, each about 140 g (5 oz)*

Salt or salt substitute *to taste*

Ground black pepper *to taste*

Olive oil *2 tsp*

Black tea leaves *60 g (2 oz), chopped*

Chives *45 g (1¹/₂ oz), finely chopped*

EDAMAME

Edamame *120 g (4¹/₂ oz), removed from pods*

Butter *15 g (¹/₂ oz) or 1 Tbsp olive oil*

GARNISH (OPTIONAL)

Fresh herbs

Prepare citrus salsa at least 1 hour before serving. Peel citrus fruit and cut into segments or cylinders using an apple corer. Add onion, ginger, tomatoes, olive oil, coriander leaves and salt and pepper to taste. Combine and leave to stand.

Prepare rice. Bring vegetable stock to a simmer. Meanwhile, in a saucepan, sauté onion in olive oil until translucent. Add rice and stir until rice begins to clump. Add a ladle of simmering stock and stir. Cook, stirring frequently, until almost all the liquid is absorbed and rice is done. Keep warm.

Prepare sea bream. Preheat oven to 200°C (400°F). Season fish fillets with salt and pepper. Heat an ovenproof frying pan and add olive oil. When pan is hot, sear fish fillets on both sides until done. Sprinkle chopped tea leaves on fish, then bake fish for about 8 minutes, or until done. Remove from oven and sprinkle chives over fish.

Sauté edamame in butter or olive oil and season to taste.

Serve sea bream with rice, salsa and edamame. Garnish with fresh herbs.

Poached Daurade with Tofu in Green Tea Broth

Preparation Time: 1 hour   Cooking Time: 20 minutes   Serves 4

LIGHT FISH STOCK

Olive oil *50 ml (1²/₃ fl oz)*

Onion *1, peeled and quartered*

Garlic *1 head, cloves separated*

Fennel bulb *1, peeled and quartered*

Fish bones *2.3 kg (5 lb)*

White wine *500 ml (16 fl oz / 2 cups)*

Water *3.8 litres (120 fl oz / 15 cups)*

White peppercorns *6*

Star anise *2*

Bay leaves *2*

Parsley *1 sprig*

DAURADE

Dashi granules *¹/₈ tsp*

Green tea leaves *40 g (1¹/₂ oz)*

Garlic *2 cloves, peeled*

Ginger *30 g (1 oz), peeled and thinly shaved*

Daurade fillets *4, each about 140 g (5 oz), seasoned with salt and ground white pepper to taste*

TOFU, VEGETABLES AND FETTUCINE

Silken or soft tofu *120 g (4¹/₂ oz), diced*

Broccoli *8 small florets*

Chinese flowering cabbage *4 stalks*

Fettuccine *120 g (4¹/₂ oz), cooked al dente*

GARNISH (OPTIONAL)

Fried shredded ginger

Prepare fish stock. Heat olive oil and sweat onion, garlic and fennel until tender. Add fish bones and cook for several minutes, then add wine. Cook off alcohol, then add water, peppercorns, star anise, bay leaves and parsley. Bring to a boil, then lower heat and simmer for 20 minutes. Strain and reduce stock to about 2 litres (64 fl oz / 8 cups).

Prepare daurade. Return fish stock to boil, then turn off heat. Add dashi granules and tea leaves. Let stand for 15 minutes, then strain and return stock to a boil. Add garlic and ginger, then turn heat to low and simmer. Add seasoned fish and poach for 4 minutes. Remove fish and divide into serving bowls.

Return fish stock to a boil. Add tofu and vegetables and cook for 4 minutes. Add fettuccine and cook until heated through. Divide fettuccine, tofu and vegetables into prepared serving bowls. Ladle stock over and garnish with shredded ginger.

Branzino Fillet Stuffed with Green Passion Tea-Flavoured Sticky Rice

Preparation Time: 45 minutes   Cooking Time: 30 minutes   Serves 4

TEA INFUSION

Water *1 litre (32 fl oz / 4 cups)*

Green passion tea leaves *30 g (1 oz)*

STICKY RICE

Short-grain rice *500 g (1 lb 1¹/₂ oz)*

Salt or salt substitute *to taste*

EDAMAME PURÉE

Unsalted Plugra butter *30 g (1 oz)*

Salt or salt substitute *to taste*

Ground black pepper *to taste*

Edamame *225 g (8 oz), blanched and drained from pods*

BRANZINO FILLETS

Vegetable oil *2 Tbsp*

Branzino fillets *16, each about 110 g (4 oz)*

VEGETABLES AND MUSHROOMS

Vegetable oil *2 Tbsp*

Brown honshimeji mushrooms *250 g (9 oz), trimmed*

Baby bok choy *12, blanched*

Edamame *500 g (1 lb 1¹/₂ oz), blanched and drained*

Shallots *2, peeled and finely minced*

Garlic *2 cloves, peeled and minced*

Preheat oven to 200°C (400°F).

Prepare tea infusion. Bring water to a boil. Add tea leaves and steep for 4 minutes. Allow tea to cool completely.

Prepare sticky rice. Using a medium saucepan, add rice, 750 ml (24 fl oz / 3 cups) tea infusion and a pinch of salt. Bring to a boil over high heat, then turn heat to low. Cover and simmer for 20 minutes or until liquid is absorbed. Keep warm.

While rice is cooking, prepare edamame purée. Measure out 175 ml (6 fl oz / ³/₄ cup) remaining tea infusion and bring to a boil in a small saucepan. Add butter, salt and pepper to taste. Add edamame, then blend mixture into a purée. Set aside for garnish.

Prepare Branzino fillets. Heat a frying pan over high heat. Add half the oil and continue to heat until oil just begins to smoke. Season fish with salt to taste, then fry skin side down until skin is crisp and golden brown. Turn fish over and sear other side. Remove fish and place on a shallow baking tray lined with greaseproof paper. Spoon warm rice over flesh side of one piece of fish. Place another fillet, flesh side down, to cover rice, making a sandwich. Continue until you have 8 sandwiches. Place in oven for 3–5 minutes.

Prepare vegetables and mushrooms. Place a frying pan or wok over high heat. Add oil and sauté mushrooms for 1 minute. Add baby bok choy, edamame, shallots and garlic and cook lightly.

Serve Branzino fillets with sautéed vegetables and mushrooms and edamame tea purée. Garnish as desired. Serve immediately.

Line-Caught Turbot with Lemon Verbena Foam
Preparation Time: 1 hour 30 minutes Cooking Time: 30 minutes Serves 4

CAPER-RAISIN CHUTNEY

Capers *40 g (1¹/₂ oz)*

Golden raisins *250 g (9 oz)*

Sherry vinegar *65 ml (2 fl oz / 4 Tbsp)*

Freshly squeezed orange juice *500 ml (16 fl oz / 2 cups)*

LEMON VERBENA FOAM

Fresh lemon verbena leaves *15 g (¹/₂ oz)*

Water *250 ml (8 fl oz / 1 cup)*

Soy lecithin (see Glossary) *¹/₄ tsp*

Salt or salt substitute *to taste*

TURBOT

Skinless turbot fillets *4, each about 120 g (4¹/₂ oz)*

Salt or salt substitute *to taste*

Olive oil *1 Tbsp*

Butter *15 g (¹/₂ oz) or use another 1 Tbsp olive oil*

Thyme *5 sprigs*

SPINACH

Baby spinach *300 g (11 oz)*

Olive oil *2 tsp*

Salt or salt substitute *to taste*

Prepare chutney. Combine all ingredients in a saucepan and bring to a boil. Lower heat and simmer until liquid is reduced by three-quarters. The resulting mixture should have the consistency of a thick syrup. Set aside at room temperature.

Prepare foam. Bring a small pot of water to a boil and blanch lemon verbena leaves for 30 seconds. Drain and immediately plunge leaves into a bowl of iced water. Drain, then purée leaves with 250 ml (8 fl oz / 1 cup) water. Strain purée through a fine-mesh sieve into a small saucepan. Stir in soy lecithin and season with salt to taste. Keep warm.

Prepare turbot. Season fish fillets with salt. Heat a large frying pan over medium heat. Add olive oil, then carefully add fillets and cook for 1–2 minutes. Shake pan often to avoid fillets sticking to pan. Turn fillets over and add butter or olive oil and thyme. Tilt pan slightly and, using a spoon, scoop up pan juices and baste fillets while cooking for another 1–2 minutes, or until just done. Remove to serving plates.

Prepare spinach. Heat olive oil in a frying pan and sauté baby spinach lightly. Season with salt to taste. Place spinach on paper towels to remove excess water.

Using a hand-held blender, blend emulsion until a frothy and airy appearance is achieved (see Kitchen Techniques).

Serve fish with chutney and spinach, topped with lemon-verbena foam.

Slow-Cooked Salmon with Jasmine Tea Jelly and Potato Dressing

Preparation Time: 3 hours   Cooking Time: 30 minutes   Serves 4

SALMON

Skinless salmon fillet *500 g (1 lb 1¹/₂ oz)*

Lemon oil *2 Tbsp*

Lemon *1, grated for zest*

Salt or salt substitute *to taste*

Ground black pepper *to taste*

WHITE JASMINE VINEGAR

White balsamic vinegar *60 ml (2 fl oz / 4 Tbsp)*

Jasmine tea leaves *15 g (¹/₂ oz)*

JASMINE TEA JELLY

Water *400 ml (13 fl oz)*

Jasmine tea leaves *8 g (¹/₃ oz)*

Gelatine sheets *6 leaves or 4¹/₂ tsp gelatine powder*

Elderflower cordial *2 tsp*

JASMINE TEA POTATO DRESSING

Vegetable oil *¹/₂ Tbsp*

Onions *50 g (2 oz), peeled and chopped*

Potatoes *500 g (1 lb 1¹/₂ oz), peeled and diced*

Chicken stock (see pg 178) *1 litre (32 fl oz / 4 cups), defatted*

Ground nutmeg *240 g (8¹/₂ oz)*

Salt or salt substitute *to taste*

Ground black pepper *to taste*

GARNISH (OPTIONAL)

Purple potatoes

Yellow potatoes

Seasonal salad greens

Chives

Salmon roe

Prepare white jasmine vinegar beforehand. Bring vinegar to a boil in a saucepan. Add tea leaves and remove from heat. Cover pan and leave for 10 minutes. Strain vinegar into a bowl and discard leaves. Set white jasmine vinegar aside.

Cut salmon into 4 equal servings. Season with lemon oil, lemon zest and salt and pepper to taste. Place in a deep baking dish and cover with plastic wrap. Set aside for 1 hour. When salmon is almost ready, preheat oven to 130°C (266°F). Remove plastic wrap from baking dish and slow-cook salmon in oven for 15 minutes. Set aside.

Prepare jasmine tea jelly. Heat water to 70°C (155°F) and pour over tea leaves. Cover and steep for 5 minutes. Strain and discard leaves. Dissolve gelatine sheets or powder in warm tea, then leave mixture to cool. Stir in elderflower cordial, then pour mixture into a wide, shallow dish so jelly is only 0.2-cm (¹/₈-in) high. Refrigerate for 2 hours or until fully set. When set, cut jelly sheet into 4 pieces.

Prepare potato dressing. Heat oil in a large pan and sauté onions until translucent. Add potatoes, chicken stock and nutmeg. Cook potatoes until tender, then purée mixture and pass through a sieve. If necessary, adjust thickness with more chicken stock and season with white jasmine vinegar and salt and pepper to taste.

Prepare potatoes for garnish. Boil potatoes until tender, then cut into cylindrical shapes using an apple corer.

Serve salmon at room temperature with potato dressing and jasmine tea jelly. Garnish with purple and yellow potatoes, salad greens, chives and salmon roe.

Shellfish

The Peninsula chefs span a wide range of cultures in the shellfish dishes chosen. For starters, there is a rustic seafood hotpot with a lively flavoured Filipino-Spanish escabeche. Then there are those dishes influenced by classical Chinese ingredients and methods of preparation. You will find from the following recipes that we open the door to bold flavours, hence the inclusion of the likes of Thai-style prawns that include lemongrass in every stage of preparation, and roasted mussels that take very little time to make. The use of healthy, healing teas such as whole green tea, and herbal lemongrass, reflect a health-conscious, delicious diversity.

Grilled Tiger Prawns with Lemongrass Tea

Preparation Time: 45 minutes   Cooking Time: 15 minutes   Serves 4

TIGER PRAWNS

Tiger prawns *24, peeled*

Lemongrass (see Glossary) *8–24 stalks or 8–24 bamboo skewers*

MARINADE

Strong lemongrass tea infusion *100 ml (3¹/₂ fl oz), cooled*

Lemongrass (see Glossary) *100 g (3¹/₂ oz) , hard outer leaves removed and chopped*

Shallots *100 g (3¹/₂ oz), peeled and chopped*

Garlic *100 g (3¹/₂ oz), peeled and chopped*

Black peppercorns *1 Tbsp*

Light soy sauce *120 ml (4 fl oz / ¹/₂ cup)*

Palm sugar *50 g (2 oz), crumbled*

SAUCE

Tamarind juice *100 ml (3¹/₂ fl oz)*

Palm sugar *100 g (3¹/₂ fl oz)*

Fish sauce *50 ml (2 fl oz)*

Chilli powder *1 Tbsp*

Lemongrass (see Glossary) *2 stalks, hard outer leaves removed and pounded*

GARNISH

Chopped red chilli

Coriander leaves or fennel leaves

Prepare marinade. Combine cooled tea, lemongrass, shallots, garlic and black peppercorns in a blender and process to a paste. You may also pound the mixture in a granite mortar and pestle. Place in a bowl with prawns. Add soy sauce and palm sugar and mix well. Leave at room temperature for 10–15 minutes.

Meanwhile, prepare tiger prawns. Trim whole stalks of lemongrass of outer leaves to make skewers, each about 8-cm (3-in) long. Alternatively, use purchased bamboo skewers. Preheat grill. Skewer 1–3 prawns onto each lemongrass stalk or bamboo skewer. Grill over medium heat for about 4 minutes until cooked.

Prepare sauce. In a small saucepan, combine ingredients for sauce and bring to a boil, stirring for about 10 minutes. Leave to cool.

Drizzle prawns with sauce and garnish with chopped chilli and herbs.

Vanilla and Black Tea Seafood Pot with Escabeche

Preparation Time: 1 hour   Cooking Time: 30 minutes   Serves 4

MUSSEL STOCK

Olive oil *2 tsp*

Shallots *40 g (1¹/₂ oz), peeled and chopped*

Green lip mussels *15, cleaned*

White wine *60 ml (2 fl oz / 4 Tbsp)*

Fish stock (see pg 179) *400 ml (13 fl oz)*

Saffron threads *1 tsp*

Vanilla tea leaves *20 g (²/₃ oz)*

SEAFOOD

Green lip mussels *8*

Clams *12*

Tiger prawns *8, peeled, leaving tails intact*

Marsh crabs *4*

Sea bass *160 g (6 oz), cut into 3-cm (1-in) pieces*

Salmon *80 g (3 oz), cut into 3-cm (1-in) pieces*

Scallops *4*

POTATOES AND HERBS

Potatoes *120 g (4 oz), peeled and sliced, or new potatoes, cut in half*

Basil leaves *6*

Coriander leaves *4 sprigs*

ESCABECHE

Canola oil *40 ml (1¹/₂ fl oz / 3 Tbsp)*

Shallots *10 g (¹/₃ oz), peeled and chopped*

Garlic *2 cloves, peeled and thinly sliced*

Jalapeno peppers *1 tsp*

Red capsicum *20 g (²/₃ oz), cored, seeded and diced*

Yellow capsicum *20 g (²/₃ oz), cored, seeded and diced*

Carrot *20 g (²/₃ oz), peeled and diced*

Red wine vinegar *1 Tbsp*

Bay leaves *2*

Ground white pepper *1 tsp*

Tabasco sauce *1 tsp*

Tomato ketchup *1 Tbsp*

Prepare mussel stock. Heat olive oil in a pan and sauté shallots lightly, then add mussels and cover. When mussels are fully open, add white wine to deglaze. Discard any mussels that do not open. Cover for another 2 minutes, then add fish stock, saffron and tea leaves. Lower heat to a simmer and reduce stock until fragrant. Strain stock into a pot and return to a simmer.

Prepare seafood. Cook each type of seafood separately in simmering stock until just done. Mussels take about 3 minutes; clams, prawns and crabs 4–5 minutes; sea bass and salmon about 4 minutes; scallops about 2 minutes. Add potatoes and herbs when seafood is done. Cook potatoes until tender. Takes about 7 minutes. As each ingredient is cooked, divide equally into 4 serving bowls.

Prepare escabeche. Heat oil in a frying pan over medium heat. Sauté shallots, garlic and jalapeno peppers for 1–3 minutes. Add all other ingredients except for ketchup. Cook until ingredients are soft, then add tomato ketchup and cook for another 1 minute. Remove from heat and cover. Refrigerate and use when needed.

To serve, ladle simmering broth over seafood and potatoes. Drop spoonfuls of escabeche into hot broth, or serve on the side. Garnish as desired and serve immediately.

Dragonwell Tiger Prawns

Preparation Time: 20 minutes   Cooking Time: 10 minutes   Serves 4

TIGER PRAWNS

Peanut or other vegetable oil *2 litres (64 fl oz / 8 cups)*

Tiger prawns *8, about 500 g (1 lb 1¹/2 oz), shelled and deveined*

Spring onion *30 g (1 oz), sliced*

Young ginger *15 g (¹/2 oz), peeled and sliced*

Carrot *30 g (1 oz), peeled and thinly sliced*

Dried lily bulbs *30 g (1 oz), soaked to rehydrate, then drained*

Fresh Dragonwell (*Long Jing*) tea leaves *25 g (1 oz)*

Strong Dragonwell (*Long Jing*) tea infusion *125 ml (4 fl oz / ¹/2 cup)*

Sea salt *to taste*

Potato starch *a pinch, mixed with 2 Tbsp cold water*

CONDIMENT

Zhejiang black rice vinegar

If substituting dried green tea, soak leaves in warm water until leaves open. Drain and save tea leaves. There should be about 25 g (1 oz) reconstituted tea leaves. Discard water.

Prepare tiger prawns. Heat oil in a wok over high heat until about 160°C (325°F). Fry prawns for 1 minute, then remove with a slotted spoon and drain on paper towels.

Heat a clean wok and add 1 Tbsp oil used for cooking prawns. Sauté spring onion, ginger, carrot and lily bulbs, tossing constantly for 30 seconds or until fragrant. Add fresh or rehydrated tea leaves and strong tea infusion. Season to taste with sea salt. Bring to a boil over low heat for 2 minutes, then stir in potato starch mixture to thicken sauce. Toss prawns in and coat well.

Drizzle black rice vinegar over prawns and serve.

Green Passion Tea-Braised King Crab and Manila Clams

Preparation Time: 30 minutes   Cooking Time: 30 minutes   Serves 4

Water *2 litres (64 fl oz / 8 cups)*

Green passion tea leaves *55 g (2 oz)*

Lemongrass (see Glossary) *1 stalk, sliced and crushed*

Shallots *2, peeled and sliced*

Garlic *2 cloves, peeled and crushed*

Leeks *2 , white part only, julienned*

Manila clams *25 pieces*

King crab legs *900 g (2 lb)*

Carrots *4, peeled and cut into fine strips*

Yellow squash *4, peeled and cut into fine strips*

Salt or salt substitute *to taste*

Ground black pepper *to taste*

GARNISH (OPTIONAL)

Deep-fried shredded lemongrass

Passion fruit seeds

Bring water to a boil and add tea leaves, sliced and crushed lemongrass, shallots and garlic. Boil for 15 minutes, then remove from heat and strain infusion into a large saucepan. Return infusion to a boil.

Add leeks and clams, then cover and cook for 4 minutes. Add crab legs, carrots and squash. Steam for another 4 minutes or until clams open. Discard any that do not open. Adjust seasoning to taste with salt and pepper.

Dish out and garnish with deep-fried shredded lemongrass and passion fruit seeds. Serve immediately.

Mussels with Ginger and Black Tea

Preparation Time: 30 minutes   Cooking Time: 10 minutes   Serves 4

MUSSELS

Mussels *1.8 kg (4 lb)*

Garlic *4 cloves, peeled*

Ginger *30 g (1 oz), peeled*

Lemongrass (see Glossary) *1 stalk,
    hard outer leaves removed*

Butter or margarine *30 g (1 oz)*

Black tea leaves *60 g (2 oz)*

Coconut milk or soy milk *600 ml (19¹/₂ fl oz)*

Light cream *235 ml (7¹/₂ fl oz)*

Olive oil *for frying*

Sake *120 ml (4 fl oz / ¹/₂ cup)*

Salt or salt substitute *1 tsp*

GARNISH

Minced ginger

Minced garlic

Minced red chilli

Scrub and clean mussels, pulling off the stringy and stretchy "beard" as necessary.

Finely chop garlic, ginger and lemongrass and combine. Divide mixture in half. Heat butter or margarine in a pan and sweat half the ginger mixture until tender. Add tea leaves, coconut or soy milk and cream. Bring to a boil, then lower heat and simmer to infuse flavours. Strain and set aside.

Heat olive oil in another pan and sauté remaining half of lemongrass mixture. Add mussels and sake, then cook for 2–3 minutes or until alcohol has evaporated. Add strained cream, then cover and cook until mussels slightly open. Discard any that do not open. Place mussels in serving bowls and continue to reduce cream by boiling for another 2 minutes.

Serve mussels with cream sauce, garnished with minced ginger, garlic and chilli.

Poultry

Poultry can play a wide range of roles in its various identities, from delicate chicken and pheasant to darker, more assertive duck and squab, a variety of pigeon. Even stronger in flavour is the game bird quail. That is why the types of teas chosen to go with this group of dishes also span quite a range: from chamomile tea for chicken to black Ceylon tea for duck and black currant tea for squab. Many of The Peninsula chefs have chosen fruit- or floral-scented teas to complement the highly versatile types of poultry in this chapter. Enjoy exploring all the varieties of tea and the way they are used with poultry.

Pan-Roasted Squab Breast with Red Onion Compote and Black Currant Tea

Preparation Time: 1 hour   Cooking Time: 45 minutes   Serves 4

RED ONION COMPOTE

Olive oil *45 ml (1¹/₂ fl oz / 3 Tbsp)*

Red onion *1, peeled and thinly sliced*

Red wine *300 ml (10 fl oz)*

Black currant tea infusion *250 ml (8 fl oz / 1 cup)*

Brown sugar *100 g (3¹/₂ oz)*

FOIE GRAS TERRINE (OPTIONAL)

Butter *30 g (1 oz), melted*

Duck livers *240 g (8¹/₂ oz)*

Salt *1 tsp*

Ground white pepper *to taste*

Ground mixed spice (blend of cloves, cinnamon, all-spice and nutmeg) *¹/₄ tsp*

Cognac or sweet sherry *1 Tbsp*

SQUAB

Squab breasts *4, trimmed and scored*

Five-spice powder *1 tsp*

Salt or salt substitute *to taste*

Ground black pepper *to taste*

Olive oil *for searing*

Port wine *120 ml (4 fl oz / ¹/₂ cup)*

Chicken stock (see pg 178) *225 ml (7¹/₂ fl oz)*

SAUTÉED GREENS

Swiss chard *1 stalk, sliced*

Yellow frisée (see Glossary) *1 head, leaves separated*

GARNISH (OPTIONAL)

Mixed currants

Thyme leaves

Prepare compote. Heat olive oil in a pan and cook onion until caramelized. Add red wine, tea infusion and sugar, and cook stirring until reduced to the consistency of jam. Leave to cool.

Prepare foie gras terrine. Brush the inside of a 120-ml (4-fl oz / ¹/₂-cup) ramekin with butter. Let livers stand at room temperature until softened. Break up liver into medium-sized pieces. Remove any skin or veins. Place cleaned liver into a bowl and mix evenly with salt, pepper, mixed spice and cognac or sherry. Pack into prepared ramekin until about three-quarters full. Place ramekin in a deep baking dish and fill dish with hot water up to half the height of ramekin. Bake in a preheated oven at 150°C (300°F) for 15 minutes. Remove ramekin from the water and leave to cool, then refrigerate until cold. When ready to serve, run the tip of a warm knife around the inner edge of ramekin and invert foie gras onto a plate. Refrigerate until required.

Prepare squab. Season squab breasts with five-spice powder and salt and pepper to taste. In a heavy frying pan over medium heat, add just enough oil to coat the bottom. Roast squab breasts for 2 minutes on each side until golden brown. Remove to rest. Pour remaining oil out of pan and deglaze with port wine. Reduce to a syrup, then add chicken stock. Reduce by half. Set aside.

Heat some olive oil and sauté Swiss chard and frisée lightly.

Serve squab with compote, sautéed greens and foie gras, if desired. Garnish with mixed currants and thyme leaves.

Slow-Cooked Duck Breast with Celeriac Salad and Chamomile Tea Dressing

Preparation Time: 1 hour   Cooking Time: 30 minutes   Serves 4

DUCK

Whole duck breasts *4, skin removed and set aside*

Thyme *4 sprigs*

Rosemary *1 stalk*

Garlic *2 cloves, peeled*

Salt or salt substitute *a pinch*

Ground black pepper *a pinch*

Chamomile tea leaves *10 g (¹/₂ oz)*

Chicken stock (see pg 178) *100 ml (3¹/₂ fl oz), defatted*

CELERIAC SALAD

Celeriac (see Glossary) *450 g (1 lb), peeled and cut into fine strips*

Salt or salt substitute *to taste*

Ground black pepper *to taste*

Dijon mustard *1 Tbsp*

Pommery mustard *1 Tbsp*

Plain non-fat yogurt *120 ml (4 fl oz / ¹/₂ cup)*

CHAMOMILE TEA DRESSING

Water *200 ml (6¹/₂ fl oz)*

Chamomile tea flowers *20 g (²/₃ oz)*

Sugar or sugar substitute *30 g (1 oz)*

Canola oil *150 ml (5 fl oz / 10 Tbsp)*

Dijon mustard *4 tsp*

Pommery mustard *1 Tbsp*

Fresh tarragon *1 sprig, chopped*

Shallots *25 g (1 oz), peeled and chopped*

Salt or salt substitute *to taste*

Ground black pepper *to taste*

DUCK SKIN (OPTIONAL)

Duck skin (from duck breasts) *4 pieces*

Salt or salt substitute *to taste*

Ground black pepper *to taste*

GARNISH

Endive, frisée (see Glossary) or other salad leaves

Prepare duck. Preheat oven to 230°C (450°F). Place duck breasts so they fit snugly in a roasting pan. Add thyme, rosemary, garlic, salt, pepper and tea leaves. Pour chicken stock over to just cover duck. Add some water if necessary. Cover pan with aluminium foil and place in the oven for 10 minutes. Reduce oven temperature to 120°C (250°F) and cook for about 20 minutes, or until internal temperature of duck breast is 45°–50°C (113°–122°F). Remove pan from oven and remove duck from stock. Set aside to cool.

Prepare celeriac salad. Season celeriac with salt and pepper and let stand for 15 minutes. The celeriac will wilt slightly. Add remaining ingredients and season to taste. Set aside.

Prepare duck skin. Trim and clean all excess meat and fat from skin. Lightly season and place on a shallow baking sheet with 1–2-cm (¹/₂–1-in) high sides. Place another baking sheet over duck skins to weigh skins down and keep them flat while baking. Bake at 230°C (450°F) for about 15 minutes, or until golden and crisp. Remove from oven and set aside to drain on paper towels.

Prepare chamomile tea dressing. Bring water to a boil, then remove from heat. Add tea and leave to infuse for about 10 minutes. Strain and combine infusion with remaining ingredients in a blender and process until smooth and glossy. Taste and adjust seasoning.

To serve, slice each duck breast thinly. Each breast should yield 12–16 slices. Lay 6–8 slices on a flat working surface, overlapping them slightly to form a large rectangle. Spoon celeriac salad onto duck and roll up.

Drizzle duck with chamomile dressing and serve with salad leaves and crispy duck skin.

Wild Pheasant Hotpot with Sichuan Tea

Preparation Time: 1 hour 30 minutes   Cooking Time: 30 minutes   Serves 4

WILD PHEASANT HOTPOT

Chicken stock (see pg 178) *1 litre (32 fl oz / 4 cups), defatted*

Sichuan tea sachets *8*

Spring onions *200 g (7 oz), shredded*

Onion *1, peeled and sliced*

Shiitake mushrooms *120 g (4¹/₂ oz), stems removed*

Firm tofu *120 g (4¹/₂ oz), cut into rounds or cubes*

Pheasant breast *540 g (1 lb 3 oz), sliced*

Sugar or sugar substitute *30 g (1 oz)*

Light soy sauce *2 Tbsp*

Dark soy sauce *60 ml (2 fl oz / 4 Tbsp)*

Baby bok choy *4 stalks*

Bring chicken stock to a boil in a hotpot, then lower heat to medium. A tagine, Chinese clay pot or enamelled cast iron pot may also be used.

Add tea sachets, then layer in spring onions, onion, mushrooms, tofu and pheasant breast. Season with sugar and soy sauces. Cover with a lid and simmer for 10–15 minutes over medium heat.

Add baby bok choy to pot and cook lightly.

Ladle soup and ingredients into serving bowls and serve immediately.

Lavender Tea-Crusted Quail with Citrus Couscous

Preparation Time: 30 minutes   Cooking Time: 30 minutes   Serves 4

LAVENDER TEA-CRUSTED QUAIL

Quail breasts *4*

Lavender tea leaves *30 g (1 oz)*

Salt or salt substitute *to taste*

Ground black pepper *to taste*

COUSCOUS

Water *500 ml (16 fl oz / 2 cups)*

Ceylon tea leaves *30 g (1 oz)*

Olive oil *2 Tbsp*

Couscous (see Glossary) *180 g (6¹/₂ oz / 1 cup)*

Orange *1, grated for zest and segmented*

Lemon *1, grated for zest and segmented*

Blood orange *1, segmented*

Lime *1, segmented*

Fresh oregano *4 sprigs, chopped*

PESTO

Basil leaves *120 g (4¹/₂ oz)*

Pine nuts *55 g (2 oz), toasted*

Reduced-fat Parmesan cheese *30 g (1 oz), grated*

Olive oil *80 ml (2¹/₂ fl oz / ¹/₃ cup)*

Salt or salt substitute *to taste*

YOUGURT

Low-fat Greek yogurt *120 ml (4¹/₂ fl oz / ¹/₂ cup)*

Salt or salt substitute *to taste*

Ground black pepper *to taste*

Prepare quail. Season quail with tea leaves, salt and pepper. Grill quail for about 2 minutes on each side, then leave to rest for 1 minute before slicing.

Prepare couscous. Bring water to a boil and add tea leaves to infuse. Strain and discard leaves. Set aside. Heat olive oil in a pan and cook couscous lightly until brown. Add tea infusion to couscous in pan. Cook for 5–7 minutes or until couscous is tender. Leave to cool before gently tossing with half of the orange and lemon zest, citrus segments and oregano.

Prepare pesto. Combine all ingredients for pesto in a blender and process to a paste.

Prepare yogurt. Stir remaining orange and lemon zest into yogurt and taste for seasoning. Add salt and pepper to taste, if necessary.

Serve grilled quail with couscous, pesto and yogurt on the side.

Chamomile-Steamed Chicken with Snow Pea Shoots

Preparation Time: 45 minutes   Cooking Time: 45 minutes   Serves 4

CHICKEN

Strong chamomile tea infusion *200 ml (6¹/₂ fl oz)*

Whole skinless chicken breasts *4, each about 200 g (7 oz)*

Small red chillies *2 or more to taste, seeds removed and chopped*

Garlic *100 g (3¹/₂ oz), peeled and chopped*

Ginger *100 g (3¹/₂ oz), peeled and chopped*

Light soy sauce *80 ml (2¹/₂ fl oz / ¹/₃ cup)*

Oyster sauce *80 ml (2¹/₂ fl oz / ¹/₃ cup)*

SNOW PEA SHOOTS

Olive oil *1 Tbsp*

Snow pea shoots *100 g (3¹/₂ oz)*

DIPPING SAUCE

Garlic *100 g (3¹/₂ oz), peeled and chopped*

Ginger *100 g (3¹/₂ oz), peeled and chopped*

Small red chillies *2–5, sliced*

Coriander roots or stems *6, chopped*

Soy bean paste *100 g (3¹/₂ oz), mashed*

Light soy sauce *60 ml (2 fl oz / 4 Tbsp)*

Lime juice *100 ml (3¹/₂ fl oz)*

Sugar or sugar substitute *60 g (2 oz)*

GARNISH (OPTIONAL)

Crisp-fried garlic

Prepare chicken. Ensure chamomile tea is a strong brew. Cool to room temperature, then place chicken in to marinate for about 30 minutes. Remove chicken from tea and pat dry.

Combine chillies, garlic, ginger, soy sauce and oyster sauce, then add chicken to this mixture. Place chicken on a shallow steaming plate and steam over medium heat for 25–30 minutes, or until just done.

Prepare snow pea shoots. Heat olive oil in a pan and stir-fry sweet pea shoots lightly. Set aside.

Prepare dipping sauce. Combine garlic, ginger, chillies, coriander roots or stems and soy bean paste and mix well. Stir in soy sauce, lime juice and sugar.

Serve chicken with stir-fried snow pea shoots and dipping sauce. Garnish with crisp-fried garlic.

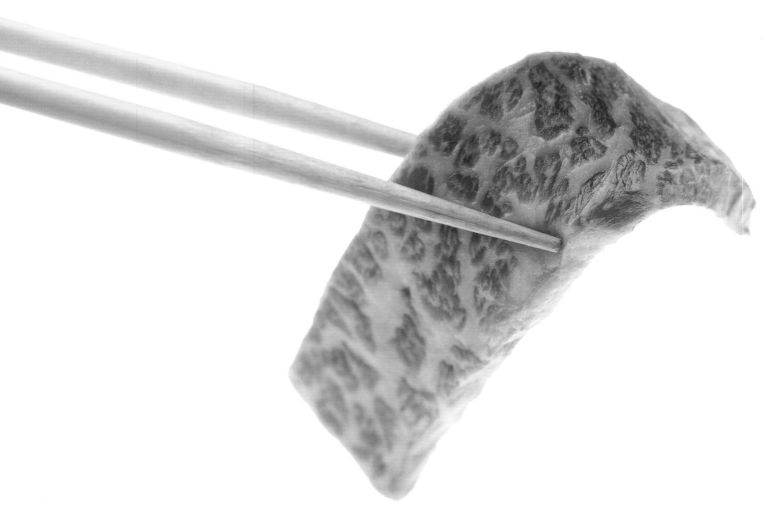

Meat

In this collection of meat dishes, you may choose from the exotic to the more familiar. This chapter spans everything from rarified Cervena venison and Wagyu beef to common pork and lamb. A correspondingly wide range of teas accents the properties of these meats; to the fore come floral, soothing chamomile (a herbal tea), smoky Lapsang Souchong and citrus-kissed Earl Grey teas.

Some Peninsula chefs choose to steep their teas and allow them to suggest their flavours in sauces. Others smoke and burn dry tea leaves so their fumes permeate the meat. Still others make a brine with tea to infuse and moisten meat gently. There is a diversity of techniques to learn and a wide range of flavours to enjoy.

Lapsang Souchong Lamb with Smoked Tea Salt

Start preparations 2 days ahead Cooking Time: 45 minutes Serves 4

TEA SALT

Lapsang Souchong tea leaves *1/4 tsp, ground into a fine powder using a spice grinder*

Fleur de sel *2 tsp*

LAMB LOIN

Lamb loin *2, each about 250 g (9 oz)*

Salt or salt substitute *a pinch*

Ground black pepper *a pinch*

Grapeseed oil *2 Tbsp*

SAUCE

Lamb stock (see pg 178) *160 ml (5 1/3 fl oz)*

Lapsang Souchong tea leaves *3 g (1/3 oz), ground into a fine powder using a spice grinder*

SWEET POTATOES

Sweet potatoes *900 g (2 lb)*

Grapeseed oil *250 ml (8 fl oz / 1 cup)*

Shallot *1, peeled and sliced*

Garlic *3 g (1/10 oz), peeled and sliced*

Bay leaf *1*

Thyme *3 sprigs*

Black peppercorns *5 g (1/6 oz)*

MUSTARD GREENS

Chinese mustard greens (see Glossary) *300 g (11 oz)*

Smoked bacon *5 slices*

Chicken stock (see pg 178) *480 ml (15 2/3 fl oz), defatted*

Freshly ground black pepper *to taste*

Salt or salt substitute *to taste*

PICKLED SHALLOTS

Shallots *2, peeled*

Red wine vinegar *375 ml (12 fl oz / 1 1/2 cups)*

Water *60 ml (2 fl oz / 4 Tbsp)*

Sugar *90 g (3 oz)*

Low sodium salt *a pinch*

Thyme *1, sprig*

Prepare tea salt 2 days ahead (see Kitchen Techniques). Let stand overnight.

Prepare lamb 1 day ahead. Trim muscle and fat off lamb loin and coat with tea salt. Cover lamb with plastic wrap and refrigerate overnight.

Preheat oven to 200°C (400°F).

Season lamb with salt and pepper. Heat oil in an ovenproof pan and brown lamb over high heat. Turn lamb over to sear all sides evenly. Transfer lamb to the oven and roast until the internal temperature of lamb is medium rare, about 52°C (125°F), or done to your preference.

Prepare sauce. Heat lamb stock in a small pot. Add ground Lapsang Souchong tea leaves and let steep for 5 minutes. Strain sauce and set aside.

Prepare sweet potatoes. Preheat oven to 120°C (250°F). Peel and cut sweet potatoes into 0.5-cm (1/4-in) thick slices. Using a 4 cm (1 1/2 in) diameter cookie cutter, cut out disks from sweet potatoes. Place in a small ovenproof saucepan and cover with grapeseed oil. Add shallot, garlic, bay leaf, thyme and black peppercorns, then place in the oven for 20 minutes or until sweet potato slices are fork tender.

Prepare pickled shallots. Cut shallots into 0.25-cm (1/8-in) thick slices and place into a small saucepan. Add vinegar, water, sugar, salt and thyme and bring to a boil. Remove from heat and let shallots cool in pickling liquid.

Prepare mustard greens. Roughly chop mustard greens. In a large saucepan, cook bacon over low heat for 5 minutes, rendering fat. Remove bacon and add mustard greens and chicken stock to pan. Cook over low heat until mustard greens are tender. Season with salt and pepper to taste.

Slice lamb and serve with sweet potatoes, pickled shallots and mustard greens. Drizzle with sauce and sprinkle with tea salt.

Earl Grey-Smoked Pork Loin

Start preparations 1 day ahead   Cooking Time: 30 minutes   Serves 4

LENTILS

French green lentils or lentilles du Puy *180 g (6¹/₂ oz)*

Olive oil *for panfrying*

Shallots *20 g (²/₃ oz)*

Vegetable stock (see pg 179) *400 ml (13 fl oz)*

PORK LOIN

Earl Grey tea leaves *50 g (2 oz)*

Mandarin zest *5 g (¹/₆ oz)*

Pork loin *640 g (1 lb 6¹/₂ oz)*

Salt or salt substitute *to taste*

Ground black pepper *to taste*

Vegetable oil *for searing*

CELERY AND LEEK

Olive oil *for panfrying*

Celery *30 g (1 oz), finely sliced*

Leek *30 g (1 oz), finely sliced*

Salt or salt substitute *to taste*

Ground black pepper *to taste*

MOREL SAUCE

Fresh morel mushrooms *30 g (1 oz)*

Veal stock (see pg 178) *170 ml (6 fl oz / ³/₄ cup)*

Prepare lentils the day before. Cover lentils with cold water, such that water rises at least 2-cm (1-in) above lentils. Leave to soak overnight.

Prepare to smoke pork. Soak Earl Grey tea leaves in cold water for 10 minutes, then strain and mix with mandarin zest. Place into a cooking pan and smoke pork for 10 minutes (see Kitchen Techniques).

Preheat oven to 180°C (350°F). Season smoked pork loin with salt and pepper. Heat oil in an ovenproof pan and sear pork on all sides. Place pan in the oven for 4–6 minutes, or until pork reaches 75°C (167°F) on an instant-read internal meat thermometer. You may wish to cook it longer to medium or well-done.

In the meantime, drain lentils. Heat a pan and add olive oil. Sauté shallots until softened. Add lentils and cook for 5 minutes, then add vegetable stock. Bring to a boil, then lower heat and simmer until cooked and stock is absorbed. Set aside and keep warm.

Prepare celery and leek just before serving. Heat a clean pan and add olive oil. Panfry celery and leek until done but still crisp. Season with salt and pepper to taste.

Prepare morel sauce. Using the same pan, cook morels, then add veal stock. Simmer until stock is heated through.

Slice pork and serve with lentils, celery and leek mixture and morel sauce. Garnish as desired.

Wagyu Beef Striploin with Lapsang Souchong Tea and Aubergine Tart

Preparation Time: 30 minutes   Cooking Time: 1 hour   Serves 4

Brussels sprouts *16*

Wagyu beef striploin *170 g (6 oz), trimmed*

TEA SALT

Lapsang Souchong tea leaves *55 g (2 oz), crushed*

Juniper berries *30 g (1 oz), crushed*

Salt or salt substitute *30 g (1 oz)*

Cracked black pepper *30 g (1 oz)*

AUBERGINE TART

Aubergine *1*

Salt or salt substitute *to taste*

Olive oil *for drizzling*

Katafi pastry *1 pack, 450 g (1 lb)*

SAUCE

Butter or margarine *30 g (1 oz)*

Onion *30 g (1 oz), peeled and sliced*

Garlic *30 g (1 oz), peeled and chopped*

Green peppercorns *¹/₂ tsp*

Bay leaf *1*

Brandy *2 Tbsp*

Red wine *250 ml (8 fl oz / 1 cup)*

Veal stock (see pg 178) *1 litre (32 fl oz / 4 cups)*

Bitter or semi-sweet chocolate *30 g (1 oz)*

GARNISH (OPTIONAL)

Garlic flowers

Prepare tea salt (see Kitchen Techniques). Dust beef liberally with tea salt and set aside.

Prepare aubergine tart. Preheat oven to 150°C (300°F). Cut aubergine in half lengthwise. Score and season with salt, then drizzle with olive oil and bake for 30 minutes or until soft. Leave to cool, then scoop out flesh and purée in a blender. Season to taste with salt and set aside.

On a baking pan, form 4 circles using katafi pastry. Drizzle with olive oil and weigh down with another baking sheet. Bake at 150°C (300°F) for about 5 minutes. Set aside.

Meanwhile, prepare Brussels sprouts. Trim bottom off Brussels sprouts and separate leaves. Blanch in boiling salted water, then drain and plunge into ice water. Drain and set aside.

Prepare sauce. Heat butter or margarine in a pan and caramelize onion and garlic. Add peppercorns, bay leaf and brandy, cooking until alcohol is evaporated. The alcohol may flame up. If so, allow it to cook through and die down. Add wine and boil down by half. Add veal stock and cook until reduced by half. Remove from heat and strain sauce, then whisk in chocolate.

Prepare beef. Preheat oven to 220°C (440°F). Coat an ovenproof pan with olive oil and pan-sear beef until golden and charred on all sides. Transfer pan to the oven and bake for about 8 minutes, until an instant-read internal meat thermometer inserted into beef reads medium rare, about 50°C (120°F). Remove beef from oven and cover loosely with aluminium foil. Allow beef to rest for 5–10 minutes before slicing.

Spoon aubergine purée onto pastry circles and serve with Brussels sprouts and sliced beef. Drizzle with sauce and garnish with garlic flowers. Serve immediately.

Photograph on pg 86–87

Salt-Baked Veal Fillet with Chamomile Cream

Start preparations 6 hours ahead   Cooking Time: 45 minutes   Serves 4

Veal fillet *500 g (1 lb 1¹/₂ oz), trimmed*

Wild mushrooms *240 g (8¹/₂ oz)*

Angel hair or fine whole wheat pasta *240 g (8¹/₂ oz)*

CEYLON TEA

Water *1 litre (32 fl oz / 4 cups)*

Ceylon tea leaves *20 g (²/₃ oz)*

SALT CRUST

Cake flour *170 g (6 oz)*

Table salt *150 g (5¹/₃ oz)*

Egg *1*

Water *100 ml (3¹/₂ fl oz)*

CHAMOMILE CREAM

Vegetable oil *4 tsp*

Shallot *10 g (¹/₃ oz), peeled and chopped*

Chicken bones *100 g (3¹/₂ oz)*

White wine *50 g (2 oz)*

Chicken stock (see pg 178) *400 ml (13 fl oz), defatted*

Light whipping cream *2 Tbsp + 4 tsp, whipped*

Chamomile petals *10 g (¹/₃ oz)*

Butter or margarine *20 g (²/₃ oz), softened*

Prepare Ceylon tea. Heat water to 70°C (155°F) and add tea leaves. Cover and allow to steep for 5 minutes. Strain and discard leaves. Allow tea infusion to cool. Place veal in cooled Ceylon tea, cover tightly and refrigerate for 6 hours.

When veal is almost ready, prepare salt crust. Combine all ingredients and form into two flat disks. Allow dough to rest for 20 minutes. Preheat oven to 240°C (465°F). Roll each piece of dough into a 0.4-cm (¹/₄-in) thick sheet. Place marinated veal in the centre of one sheet of dough, then cover with other sheet of dough. Press edges together, sealing veal in tightly. Trim edges and bake for about 10 minutes or until an instant-read internal meat thermometer inserted into veal reads 60°C (140°F). Remove from oven and leave to cool for about 5 minutes.

Prepare chamomile cream. While veal is in oven, heat oil and sauté shallot and chicken bones until bones are golden brown in colour. Deglaze with white wine, then add chicken stock and simmer until liquid is reduced by half. Add 2 Tbsp cream and chamomile petals to reduced stock. Bring to a boil and adjust seasoning to taste. Simmer for 1 minute, then strain through a fine sieve and discard petals. Just before serving, add butter and fold in 4 tsp whipped cream. Taste and adjust seasoning.

While waiting for chamomile cream to reduce, sauté mushrooms and cook pasta according to packet instructions.

To serve, cut open salt crust and slice veal. Serve veal with mushrooms and pasta. Drizzle with chamomile cream.

Photograph on pg 90–91

Orange Tea Marinated Pork Loin with Cranberry Sauce and Apple Fondant

Start preparations 1–2 days ahead   Cooking Time: 1 hour 30 minutes   Serves 4

ORANGE TEA PORK LOIN

Lemons *2*

Strong orange tea infusion *1.25 litres (40 fl oz / 5 cups)*

Sugar or sugar substitute *140 g (5 oz)*

Kosher salt *60 g (2 oz)*

Iced water *1 litre (32 fl oz / 4 cups)*

Organic pork loin *700 g (1¹/₂ lb), trimmed*

Canola oil *2 Tbsp*

Salt or salt substitute *to taste*

Ground black pepper *to taste*

CRANBERRY SAUCE

Cranberries *500 g (1 lb 1¹/₂ oz)*

Orange tea infusion *625 ml (20 fl oz / 2¹/₂ cups)*

Freshly squeezed orange juice *625 ml (20 fl oz / 2¹/₂ cups)*

Sugar or sugar substitute *140 g (5 oz)*

Oranges *2, grated for zest*

Ginger *30 g (1 oz), peeled and sliced*

Sherry vinegar *2 Tbsp*

Light maple syrup *45 ml (1¹/₂ fl oz / 3 Tbsp)*

ORANGE REDUCTION

Freshly squeezed orange juice *500 ml (16 fl oz / 2 cups)*

Sugar or sugar substitute *160 g (6 oz)*

APPLE FONDANT

Orange tea infusion *500 ml (16 fl oz / 2 cups)*

Sugar or sugar substitute *220 g (8 oz)*

Baby Fuji apples *4, peeled and cored*

Canola oil

GARNISH (OPTIONAL)

Sage leaves

Sliced cranberries

Fleur de sel mixed with orange tea leaves

Prepare pork loin 1–2 days before cooking. Zest and quarter lemons, then place in a saucepan with tea infusion, sugar and salt. Simmer mixture over medium-high heat until sugar and salt dissolve. Add iced water and submerge pork in this brine. Refrigerate for 1–2 days.

On the day of cooking, prepare cranberry sauce. Place cranberries, tea infusion, orange juice and sugar in a medium saucepan. Wrap orange zest and ginger in a piece of cheesecloth and place in saucepan. Cook over low heat for 45 minutes to 1 hour, being careful that mixture does not burn on the bottom of pot. When sauce forms a homogenous mixture, stir in vinegar and maple syrup. Keep warm.

Prepare orange reduction. Heat orange juice and sugar in a small saucepan until reduced by half. Strain and leave to cool.

Prepare apple fondant. Heat tea infusion and sugar in a saucepan over low heat. Once sugar dissolves, add apples. Poach until soft, but still firm in the centre, about 10 minutes. Cool and set aside. Reserve poaching liquid. Just before serving, heat a small pan with canola oil. Add apples and brown, turning apples as they cook. Add 250 ml (8 fl oz / 1 cup) reserved poaching liquid to pan and continue to cook apples, turning them over until liquid has thickened. This takes about 20 minutes. Remove from heat and cut into desired shapes.

Prepare pork. Preheat oven to 180°C (350°F). Remove pork from brine and pat dry. Heat a large sauté pan with canola oil. Season pork with salt and pepper to taste, then cook on all sides until caramelized. Takes about 3 minutes for each side. Transfer to the oven and bake until internal temperature of pork is 55°C (130°F) on an instant-read meat thermometer. Takes about 6 minutes. Set meat aside to rest for 5–10 minutes before slicing. It will be pink in the middle. Cook pork longer, if preferred.

Slice pork and serve with cranberry sauce, orange reduction and apple fondant. Garnish with sage leaves, sliced cranberries and fleur de sel mixed with orange tea leaves.

Roasted Venison with Himalayan Tea Leaves

Preparation Time: 2 hours 30 minutes   Cooking Time: 30 minutes   Serves 4

ROASTED VENISON

Himalayan tea leaves *90 g (3 oz)*

Rosemary *0.5 g, chopped*

Thyme *0.5 g, chopped*

Cervena venison loin *540 g (1 lb 3 oz), trimmed*

Salt or salt substitute *to taste*

Ground black pepper *to taste*

Canola oil *2 tsp*

Veal stock (see pg 178) *60 ml (2 fl oz / 4 Tbsp)*

LEEKS

Chicken stock (see pg 178) *2 Tbsp*

Olive oil *1 Tbsp*

Kujo leeks *120 g (4¹/₂ oz), cut into 7.5-cm (3-in) lengths*

Garlic *10 g (¹/₃ oz), peeled*

Star anise *1*

Salt or salt substitute *to taste*

Ground black pepper *to taste*

BABY FENNEL

Baby fennel *2 bulbs*

Olive oil *1 Tbsp*

Salt or salt substitute *to taste*

Ground black pepper *to taste*

CHERRIES

Cherries *4, stone removed and halved*

Light maple syrup *1 Tbsp*

GARNISH

Fresh herbs

Prepare venison. Using a spice grinder, grind dry tea leaves with fresh rosemary and thyme into a fine powder. Season venison with salt and pepper, then roll in tea-rosemary-thyme powder.

Preheat oven to 230°C (450°F). Heat canola oil in an ovenproof pan over high heat and sear venison on all sides. Place in the oven for about 8 minutes for medium-rare or cook to your preferred doneness. Remove venison and let rest for about 4 minutes.

Prepare leeks. In a small saucepan, heat chicken stock and olive oil on high. Add leeks, garlic and star anise. Bring to a boil, then braise leeks over medium heat, covered, for about 15 minutes. Season with salt and pepper to taste.

Prepare baby fennel. Cut baby fennel in half and place into a roasting pan. Drizzle with olive oil, salt and pepper. Cook in an oven preheated to 230°C (450°F) for 20 minutes or until tender.

Prepare cherries. In a small sauté pan, cook cherries with maple syrup over low heat for 8–10 minutes or until well-coated and softened.

Reheat veal stock.

Slice venison and serve with leeks, roasted fennel and cherries. Drizzle with reheated veal stock and garnish with fresh herbs.

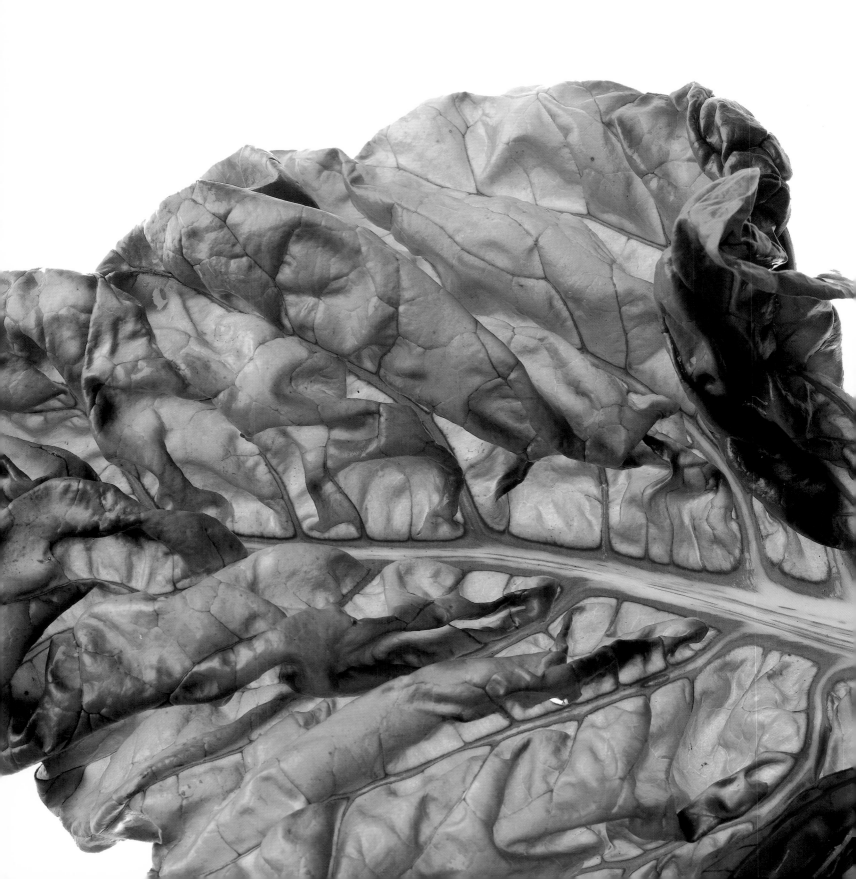

Vegetables and Tofu

Vegetables and tofu are the most subtle of ingredients. They can absorb and exhibit the various aromas of tea transparently and cleanly. The chefs of all the Peninsula properties have used teas such as chrysanthemum, lemon verbena and cherry blossom to go with their treatment of these ingredients. Cuisines range from traditional Chinese to French and Japanese, and many of the following dishes are vegetarian main courses in themselves rather than accompaniments to other dishes. Enjoy them as light meals, knowing you are eating healthily.

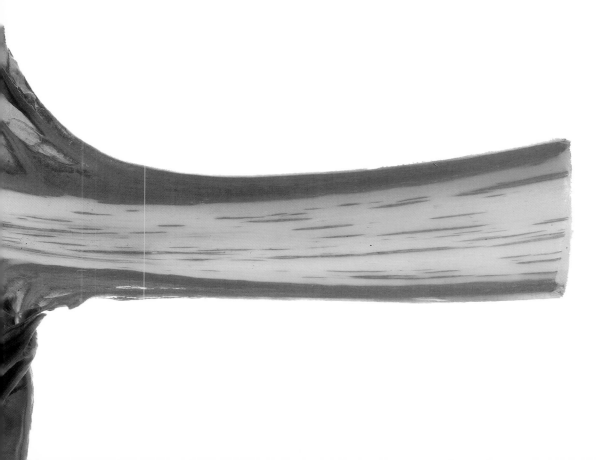

Black Tea-Smoked Tofu

Start preparations 2 hours ahead   Cooking Time: 1 hour   Serves 4

TEA OIL

Vegetable oil *60 ml (2 fl oz / 4 Tbsp)*

Black tea leaves *15 g (¹/₂ oz)*

PEANUT SAUCE

Peanuts *250 g (9 oz), finely ground*

Bird's eye chillies *30 g (1 oz), seeds removed*

Sugar or sugar substitute *20 g (²/₃ oz)*

Lime juice *2 Tbsp*

Tamarind juice *40 ml (1¹/₂ fl oz / 3 Tbsp)*

Light soy sauce *1 Tbsp*

Salt or salt substitute *to taste*

Ground white pepper *to taste*

SMOKED TOFU

Black tea leaves *60 g (2 oz)*

Firm tofu *2 slabs, each about 11 x 9-cm (4¹/₂–3¹/₂-in) and 0.2-cm (¹/₈-in) thick*

Cucumber *140 g (5 oz), seeded and cut into fine strips*

Salt or salt substitute *to taste*

Ground white pepper *to taste*

Hoisin sauce *60 ml (2 fl oz / 4 Tbsp)*

Sesame oil *2 tsp*

Coriander leaves *30 g (1 oz), chopped*

Dried bean curd skin *1 sheet, about 24 x 22-cm (9¹/₂ x 9-in)*

GARNISH

Salad greens

Prepare tea oil. Warm oil and pour over tea leaves. Leave for 2 hours, then strain and set aside.

Meanwhile, prepare peanut sauce. Purée ingredients for peanut sauce in a blender, adding a little water if necessary to achieve a smooth paste. Set aside.

Prepare smoked tofu. Soak tea leaves in some water, then drain and use to smoke tofu for 3–5 minutes (see Kitchen Techniques). Remove tofu and cut into 4 thin slabs. Combine cucumber strips with salt, pepper, hoisin sauce, sesame oil and coriander leaves. Wipe dried bean curd skin with a damp cloth and arrange tofu slabs side by side on bean curd skin. Spoon cucumber mixture over and roll up, using bean curd skin to hold roll together. Cut roll into 4 pieces.

Drizzle rolls with tea oil and serve with peanut sauce. Garnish with salad greens.

Kadai Tofu

Preparation Time: 30 minutes   Cooking Time: 15 minutes   Serves 4

KADAI TOFU

Corn oil *60 ml (2 fl oz / 4 Tbsp)*

Cumin seeds *a pinch*

Ginger *10 g (¹/₃ oz), peeled and chopped*

Garlic *10 g (¹/₃ oz), peeled and chopped*

Red capsicum *60 g (2 oz), cored, seeded and diced*

Green capsicum *60 g (2 oz), cored, seeded and diced*

Onion *90 g (3 oz), peeled and diced*

Tomato *60 g (2 oz), diced*

Firm tofu *200 g (7 oz), diced*

Tomato paste *30 g (1 oz)*

Coriander leaves *1 sprig, chopped*

Cayenne pepper *a pinch*

Crushed black pepper *a pinch*

Salt or salt substitute *a pinch*

Darjeeling tea infusion *120 ml (4 fl oz / ¹/₂ cup)*

GARNISH

Dried red chilli powder

Heat corn oil in a pan over medium heat. Sauté cumin seeds, ginger and garlic until aromas are released.

Add red and green capsicums, onion and tomato and stir-fry for 3–4 minutes. Add tofu, tomato paste, coriander leaves, cayenne pepper, black pepper, salt and tea infusion. Cook for another 3–4 minutes.

Serve tofu garnished with dried red chilli powder.

Earl Grey-Marinated Tofu with Summer Vegetables

Preparation Time: 45 minutes   Cooking Time: 30 minutes   Serves 4

TOFU

Firm white tofu *300 g (11 oz), cut into 4 rounds, each about 1-cm (^{1}/$_2$-in) thick (set remaining tofu bits aside for cooking with vegetables)*

Earl Grey tea infusion *450 ml (15 fl oz)*

Vegetable stock (see pg 179) *60 ml (2 fl oz / 4 Tbsp)*

Light soy sauce *60 ml (2 fl oz / 4 Tbsp)*

Brown sugar *60 g (2 oz)*

Rice wine vinegar *60 ml (2 fl oz / 4 Tbsp)*

Garlic *90 g (3 oz), peeled and chopped*

Shallots *90 g (3 oz), peeled and chopped*

Spring onion *1, cut into short lengths*

Black and white sesame seeds *for coating*

VEGETABLES

Olive oil *for frying*

Carrots *150 g (5^1/$_3$ oz), peeled and cut into fine strips*

Leeks *150 g (5^1/$_3$ oz), cut into fine strips*

Red capsicums *250 g (9 oz), cored, seeded and cut into fine strips*

Green capsicums *250 g (9 oz), cored, seeded and cut into fine strips*

Yellow capsicums *250 g (9 oz), cored, seeded and cut into fine strips*

Sweet potato *90 g (9 oz), peeled and cut into fine strips*

Cherry tomatoes *100 g (3^1/$_2$ oz)*

Salt or salt substitute *to taste*

Ground white pepper *to taste*

GARNISH

Finely shredded spring onion

In a non-reactive bowl, submerge tofu in mixture of tea infusion, stock, soy sauce, brown sugar, rice wine vinegar, garlic, shallots and spring onion for 20 minutes.

Preheat oven to 180°C (350°F). Remove tofu, pat dry with paper towels, then coat flat sides with sesame seeds. In an ovenproof pan heated with oil, sear each side of tofu, then place into oven for 3 minutes.

Heat olive oil in a pan and sauté each vegetable separately. Set aside. Cut remaining tofu bits into small cubes and sauté. Toss sautéed vegetables and tofu cubes together with salt and pepper to taste.

Serve tofu with vegetables on the side. Garnish with shredded spring onion.

Bamboo Shoots and Tofu in Sakura Tea Broth

Preparation Time: 30 minutes   Cooking Time: 15 minutes   Serves 4

TEA STOCK

Water *300 ml (10 fl oz / 1¹/₄ cups)*

Sweet Sakura tea leaves *30 g (1 oz)*

Kikkoman soy sauce *4 tsp*

Aji-mirin *2 Tbsp*

BAMBOO SHOOTS AND TOFU

Bamboo shoots *60 g (2 oz), cut into strips*

Carrot *80 g (3 oz), peeled and cut into strips*

Lotus root *40 g (1¹/₂ oz), sliced*

Shiitake mushrooms *70 g (2¹/₂ oz), sliced*

Sugar snap peas *50 g (1²/₃ oz)*

Soft or silken tofu *50 g (1²/₃ oz), cut into cubes*

Prepare tea stock. Bring water to a boil, then remove from heat. Add tea leaves and leave to sit for 30 minutes. Strain infusion and add soy sauce and mirin to balance the sweetness and saltiness, adjusting to taste as needed.

Bring tea stock to a gentle simmer and poach bamboo shoots, carrot, lotus root, mushrooms and sugar snap peas separately. Poach tofu last.

Drizzle a small quantity of tea stock over poached ingredients and serve.

Tea-Smoked Aubergine Cannelloni with Pine Nut-Golden Raisin Chutney

Preparation Time: 4 hours   Cooking Time: 45 minutes   Serves 4

AUBERGINE CHUTNEY

Aubergine *250 g (9 oz) peeled and cut into 1-cm (¹/₂-in) cubes*

Tie guan yin tea leaves *50 g (1²/₃ oz)*

Rice *50 g (1²/₃ oz)*

Sugar or sugar substitute *30 g (1 oz)*

Olive oil *75 ml (2¹/₂ fl oz / 5 Tbsp)*

Water *100 ml (3¹/₂ fl oz)*

Garlic *1, peeled and puréed*

Red chilli *1, chopped*

Cumin seeds *a pinch*

Chinese five-spice powder *a pinch*

Balsamic vinegar *50 ml (1²/₃ fl oz)*

Light maple syrup *100 ml (3¹/₂ fl oz)*

Golden raisins *75 g (2¹/₂ oz)*

Pine nuts *50 g (1²/₃ oz)*

Dijon mustard *30 g (1 oz)*

AUBERGINE WRAPS

Olive oil *for frying*

Aubergine *12 slices, each 0.5-cm (¹/₄-in) thick*

Salt or salt substitute *to taste*

AUBERGINE CHIPS (OPTIONAL)

Aubergine slices *8 thin slices, each about 0.2-cm (¹/₈-in) thick*

Olive oil *for brushing*

Salt or salt substitute *to taste*

Ground black pepper *to taste*

Prepare aubergine chips, if desired. Preheat oven to 60°C (140°F). Place aubergine slices onto greaseproof paper. Brush with olive oil and season with salt and pepper to taste. Place in oven to dry for about 4 hours. When chips are crisp, remove and leave to cool before storing in an airtight container. Alternatively, cut long thin strips of aubergine skin and dry as above.

Prepare chutney. Wrap aubergine cubes in cheesecloth and smoke with tea leaves, rice and sugar for 8 minutes (see Kitchen Techniques). Remove aubergine from pan and unwrap. Heat olive oil in a clean pan and sear smoked aubergine cubes until tender. Add water and simmer over low heat until reduced by about half, then add all remaining ingredients and bring to a boil. Taste and adjust seasoning if necessary. Remove from heat and set aside to cool.

Prepare aubergine wraps. Heat some olive oil in a pan and sear aubergine slices for 20 seconds on each side. Sprinkle with salt and pat dry. Lay an aubergine slice on a flat surface and top with some chutney. Roll up and repeat to make 12 rolls.

Serve aubergine cannelloni with excess chutney and garnish with aubergine chips.

Cauliflower Quiche with Peppermint Tea

Start preparations 1 day ahead   Cooking Time: 1 hour   Serves 4

CAULIFLOWER

Water *1.5 litres (48 fl oz / 6 cups)*

Peppermint tea leaves *1 tsp*

Cauliflower *300 g (11 oz)*

Vegetable oil *4 tsp*

Shallots *20 g (²/₃ oz), peeled and chopped*

Salt or salt substitute *to taste*

Ground black pepper *to taste*

CUSTARD

Low-fat milk *100 ml (3¹/₂ fl oz)*

Peppermint tea leaves *¹/₂ tsp*

Light whipping cream *100 ml (3¹/₂ fl oz)*

Egg *1*

Salt or salt substitute *to taste*

Ground black pepper *to taste*

TART SHELL

Organic wheat flour *250 g (9 oz)*

Butter or margarine *25 g (1 oz)*

Egg yolks *2*

Water *50 ml (1²/₃ fl oz)*

Salt or salt substitute *4 g*

Semolina

Dried beans or pie weights

NOTE

To blind bake means to partially cook the pie crust before the filling is added. Dried beans or pie weights are placed on the dough to keep it from puffing up (and weakening the crust) while baking.

Prepare cauliflower. Heat water in a saucepan to 70°C (155°F) and remove from heat. Add peppermint tea leaves, cover and allow to steep for 5 minutes. Strain tea infusion and discard leaves. Bring tea infusion to a boil and cook cauliflower until tender. Do not overcook. Heat vegetable oil and sauté shallots until translucent, then add cooked cauliflower and season with salt and pepper to taste. Set aside.

Prepare custard. Heat milk in a saucepan to 70°C (155°F) and remove from heat. Add peppermint tea leaves, cover and allow to steep for 15 minutes. Strain and discard leaves. Place pan in a bowl of iced water to cool milk. Whisk in cream, egg and salt and pepper to taste. Cover and refrigerate for 12 hours.

Prepare tart shell. Combine ingredients, except semolina and dried beans or pie weights, to form dough. Add 2 –3 tsp more water as necessary. Place dough in a bowl and cover tightly with plastic wrap. Refrigerate for 24 hours.

Preheat oven to 160°C (325°F). Place dough on a flour-dusted work surface and roll out into a 2-cm (1-in) thick sheet. Using a 20-cm (8-in) loose-bottom pan, trace and cut out a circle of greaseproof paper the same size as base of pan and set aside. Grease pan with some butter or margarine and dust with semolina. Place rolled dough into pan with some dough hanging over the edge. Prick holes in dough with a fork. Place cut greaseproof paper over dough in pan, then add dried beans or pie weights and blind bake for 10 minutes. Remove tart shell from oven and remove beans or weights and greaseproof paper. Leave to cool, then turn oven temperature up to 200°C (400°F).

Spoon cauliflower mixture onto tart shell and pour custard over. Bake quiche at 200°C (400°F) for 35 minutes, or until a knife inserted into the centre comes out clean. Remove from oven and place on a rack to cool before cutting and serving.

Spring Vegetable Pot Au Feu in Chrysanthemum Broth

Preparation Time: 30 minutes   Cooking Time: 45 minutes   Serves 4

CHRYSANTHEMUM TEA BROTH

Vegetable stock (see pg 179) *500 ml (16 fl oz / 2 cups)*

Chrysanthemum tea flowers *12–15 g ($^2/_5$–$^1/_2$ oz)*

Salt or salt substitute *to taste*

SPRING VEGETABLES

Baby turnips

Baby yellow beets

Thumbelina carrots

Daikon

Asparagus tips

Sugar snap peas

Broad beans

Red capsicums

New potatoes

Prepare chrysanthemum tea broth. Bring vegetable stock to a boil in a large pot. Remove from heat and add chrysanthemum tea flowers. Allow to steep for 2 minutes, then strain through cheesecloth. Set aside and keep warm.

Prepare vegetables. Use a total of 500 g (1 lb 1$^1/_2$ oz) vegetables. Peel and wash as necessary, then cut into smaller pieces where necessary. Bring a large pot of water to a boil and add salt. Cook each vegetable separately until just tender, then plunge into an ice-water bath to stop the cooking process. Drain well and pat dry.

Arrange vegetables in a casserole. Pour hot stock over and bake in a preheated oven at 180°C (350°F) for 5 minutes until hot. Serve home-style in bowls.

Lotus Tea Vegetable Rolls with Spicy Fruit Salsa

Preparation Time: 45 minutes   Cooking Time: 10 minutes   Serves 4

Vietnamese rice paper *4 sheets*

SEASONING

Salt or salt substitute *to taste*

Ground white pepper *to taste*

Fish sauce (optional) *to taste*

FILLING

Coriander leaves *30 g (1 oz), plucked from stems*

Fresh mushrooms *60 g (2 oz), thinly sliced*

Butter lettuce leaves *4 large leaves*

Red, green and yellow capsicums *60 g (2 oz), cored, seeded and cut into fine strips*

Cucumbers *60 g (2 oz), peeled, seeded and cut into fine strips*

Spring onions *60 g (2 oz), cut into fine strips*

Celery *60 g (2 oz), peeled, cut into fine strips*

Basil *30 g (1 oz), chopped*

Lotus tea leaves *30 g (1 oz)*

Orchid tea leaves *30 g (1 oz)*

SPICY FRUIT SALSA

Yuzu juice *1 Tbsp*

Lemon juice *1 Tbsp*

Organic honey *1 Tbsp or 15 g (¹/₂ oz) sugar substitute*

Red chilli *10 g (¹/₃ oz), finely chopped*

Tomato *90 g (3 oz), peeled and diced*

Pear *90 g (3 oz), pared and diced*

Pineapple *90 g (3 oz), peeled and diced*

Coriander leaves *15 g (¹/₂ oz), chopped*

Dip a sheet of rice paper in cold water briefly, then lay it on a damp tea towel. Place some coriander leaves on rice paper sheet, then layer with slices of mushroom, lettuce, vegetables and remaining herbs and tea leaves. Season with salt and pepper or fish sauce, then roll up. Repeat until ingredients are used up.

Prepare spicy fruit salsa. Combine all ingredients and let stand for 30 minutes.

Trim ends of rice paper rolls to neaten, then cut and serve immediately with spicy fruit salsa on the side.

White Tea-Infused Spring Vegetables with "Red Capsicum Paint"

Preparation Time: 45 minutes   Cooking Time: 30 minutes   Serves 4

VEGETABLES

Vegetable stock (see pg 179) *480 ml (16 fl oz / 2 cups)*

Peony white tea leaves *60 g (2 oz)*

Tri-colour cauliflower *240 g (8¹/₂ oz) each*

Baby squash *160 g (6 oz), cut into quarters*

Haricot vert *300 g (11 oz)*

Broccolini *180 g (6¹/₂ oz)*

Tomatoes *30 g (1 oz)*

Cherry tomatoes *80 g (3 oz)*

Butter or olive oil *1 Tbsp*

RED CAPSICUM PAINT

Large red capsicums *4, about 965 g (2 lb 2¹/₂ oz)*

Olive oil *125 ml (4 fl oz / ¹/₂ cup)*

White balsamic vinegar *5 tsp*

Salt or salt substitute *to taste*

Ground white pepper *to taste*

Bring vegetable stock to a simmer in a medium saucepan. Add tea leaves and remove from heat. Allow tea to infuse for 5 minutes. Strain and discard leaves, then bring liquid to a boil and blanch vegetables, except tomatoes, in separate batches in tea stock. Drain and set aside.

Prepare red capsicum paint. Roast whole capsicums over an open flame or grill until charred on all sides. Peel skin off and remove seeds. Rinse and ensure seeds are completely removed. Purée in a blender until smooth, then add olive oil and vinegar, and season with salt and pepper to taste.

Heat butter or olive oil in a frying pan. Sauté blanched vegetables and tomatoes lightly.

Serve vegetables with red capsicum paint.

Rice and Pasta

Rice and pasta serve the multi-faceted world of cooking with tea very well. Neutral in and of themselves, they easily become a canvas onto which the colours of tea may be painted. They at once absorb and display the flavours of jasmine, Earl Grey, chrysanthemum or Lapsang Souchong, for example. All carbohydrates being slightly sweet, the marriages of pasta and green tea, or risotto and Earl Grey, come to life on the palate.

Some of these recipes embody the idea of comfort food and are easily and quickly assembled. Others ask that you make pasta from scratch, which is simple enough with a pasta-rolling machine.

Jasmine Tea Gnocchi in Crayfish Bisque

Preparation Time: 2 hours   Cooking Time: 30 minutes   Serves 4

GNOCCHI

Russet potatoes *250 g (9 oz)*

Plain flour *75 g (2¹/₂ oz)*

Strong jasmine tea infusion *2 tsp*

Parsley *10 g (¹/₃ oz), chopped*

Grated Parmesan cheese *20 g (²/₃ oz)*

Salt or salt substitute *a pinch*

Ground black pepper *a pinch*

Egg yolks *2*

Extra virgin olive oil *1 Tbsp*

Crayfish tails *120 g (4¹/₂ oz)*

Baby corn *12, husked, blanched and cut into rounds*

Lemon juice *to taste*

Chives *a small bunch, chopped*

CRAYFISH BISQUE

Olive oil *2 Tbsp*

Crayfish heads and shells *1 kg (2 lb 3 oz)*

Garlic *2 cloves, peeled*

Onions *150 g (5¹/₃ oz), peeled and diced*

Red capsicums *150 g (5¹/₂ oz), cored, seeded and diced*

Celery *150 g (5¹/₂ oz), diced*

Ginger *10 g (¹/₃ oz)*

Madeira *200 ml (6¹/₂ fl oz)*

Brandy *200 ml (6¹/₂ fl oz)*

Tomatoes *350 g (12 oz), diced*

Vanilla bean *1, split in half*

Thyme *1 stalk*

Basil *a few sprigs*

Tarragon *1 stalk*

Butter or margarine *200 g (7 oz), cut into cubes*

GARNISH (OPTIONAL)

Micro greens

Prepare gnocchi. Preheat oven to 180°C (350°F) and bake whole potatoes for 1 hour. Peel potatoes while warm, then mash until all lumps are removed, or run potatoes through a food mill. Allow to cool. Combine mashed potatoes with flour, tea infusion, parsley, cheese, salt, pepper and egg yolks until dough is formed. Divide dough into smaller portions and roll into several long, cylindrical sticks approximately 30-cm (12-in) long each. Cut into 1-cm (¹/₂-in) pieces and shape lightly into oval shapes, then use a fork to gently press each piece to create an impression of the tines. Transfer gnocchi to a non-stick tray, sprinkle with flour and refrigerate.

Prepare crayfish bisque. Heat olive oil in a large saucepan and sauté crayfish heads, shells and garlic over high heat. Add onions, capsicums, celery and ginger and cook until onions are lightly caramelized. Add Madeira and brandy, scraping the bottom of the pan with a wooden spoon. Add tomatoes, vanilla bean and enough water to cover ingredients. Bring to a boil and cook until liquid is reduced by half. Allow bisque to boil for a few more minutes, then remove from heat and add thyme, basil and tarragon. Pass bisque through a food mill and strain. Whisk in butter or margarine until well-incorporated. This may be done ahead of time.

Just before serving, bring a large pot of water to a boil and cook gnocchi. Gnocchi will float when cooked. Drain well. Heat extra virgin olive oil in a frying pan and sauté gnocchi for 2 minutes. Add crayfish tails and baby corn and sauté for 30 seconds. Season with lemon juice and sprinkle in chives.

Reheat crayfish bisque. Serve sautéed gnocchi in bowls. Pour crayfish bisque over gnocchi and garnish with micro greens.

Vintage 1990 Pu'er Tea Risotto with Sweet Garlic Foam

Preparation Time: 1 hour   Cooking Time: 45 minutes   Serves 4

RISOTTO

Vegetable stock (see pg 179) *1.8 litres (60 fl oz / 7¹/₂ cups)*

Vintage 1990 pu'er tea leaves *10 g (¹/₂ oz)*

Olive oil *2 Tbsp*

Onions *70 g (2¹/₂ oz), small, peeled and diced*

Garlic *2 cloves, peeled and minced*

Carnaroli rice *260 g (9 oz)*

White wine *80 ml (2¹/₂ fl oz / ¹/₃ cup)*

Salt or salt substitute *a pinch*

MUSHROOMS

Seasonal wild mushrooms *140 g (5 oz)*

Olive oil *1 Tbsp*

Garlic *1 clove, peeled and minced*

Shallot *1, peeled and minced*

Thyme *1 stalk, chopped*

Salt or salt substitute *to taste*

Ground black pepper *to taste*

GARLIC FOAM (OPTIONAL)

Low-fat milk *1.5 litres (48 fl oz / 6 cups)*

Garlic *6 cloves, peeled*

Water *140 ml (5 fl oz)*

Salt or salt substitute *a pinch*

Light cream *60 ml (2 fl oz / 4 Tbsp)*

Butter or margarine *15 g (¹/₂ oz)*

GARNISH

Thyme flowers

Prepare risotto. Place vegetable stock in a large pot and bring to a simmer. Remove from heat and add tea leaves. Let steep for 10 minutes, then strain stock back into pot and simmer.

Heat a medium-size straight-sided pot over medium heat. Add olive oil, onions and garlic. Sauté, stirring constantly with a wooden spoon for 2½ minutes or until onions are translucent. Add rice and sauté for 1 minute, stirring. Add white wine and stir until wine is almost completely absorbed. Add just enough simmering stock to cover rice, then simmer over medium heat until stock is almost completely absorbed. Season with salt.

Add more stock to rice in 125 ml (4 fl oz / ¹/₂ cup) increments, stirring continuously after each addition with a wooden spoon until rice has absorbed most of the liquid but is not dry. Repeat until rice is cooked through but grains are still firm in the centre and surrounded by creamy liquid outside. This process should take 18–20 minutes.

Prepare mushrooms. Place mushrooms into a bowl of cold water and wash thoroughly 2–3 times. Remove and dry mushrooms on paper towels. Heat a pan over high heat. Add olive oil, garlic, shallot and mushrooms. Toss over high heat for 2 minutes, then add thyme. Season to taste with salt and pepper. Spoon hot mushrooms onto finished risotto.

Prepare garlic froth. Place 500 ml (16 fl oz / 2 cups) milk and garlic into a pot and simmer over low heat. Remove garlic and repeat process with a fresh change of milk two more times. Add water, salt and cream to garlic and simmer. Using a blender, process until mixture is smooth. Just before serving, add butter or margarine and blend using a hand-held blender held at the surface of the liquid to produce froth (see Kitchen Techniques).

Serve risotto with mushrooms and foam. Garnish with thyme flowers.

Beef Curry with Green Tea Noodles

Preparation Time: 45 minutes   Cooking Time: 20 minutes   Serves 4

GREEN TEA NOODLES

Matcha (green tea powder) *2 Tbsp*

Plain flour *500 g (1 lb 1^1/$_2$ oz)*

Green tea infusion *50 ml (1^2/$_3$ fl oz)*

Egg yolks *10*

Salt or salt substitute *1 tsp*

Vegetable oil *for deep-frying*

CURRY

Red curry paste *40 g (1^1/$_2$ oz)*

Curry powder *20 g (^{2}/$_3$ oz)*

Fresh coconut milk or soy milk *1 litre (32 fl oz / 4 cups)*

Light soy sauce *80 ml (2^1/$_2$ fl oz / ^{1}/$_3$ cup)*

Sugar or sugar substitute *20 g (^{2}/$_3$ oz)*

BEEF

Beef tenderloin *4 sliced portions, each about 75 g (2^1/$_2$ oz)*

Salt or salt substitute *1 tsp*

Ground black pepper *1 tsp*

CONDIMENTS

Shallots *40 g (1^1/$_2$ oz), peeled and sliced*

Pickled mustard *40 g (1^1/$_2$ oz)*

Chilli paste *4 Tbsp*

Limes *4, cut in half*

GARNISH (OPTIONAL)

Crisp-fried shallots

Coriander leaves

Prepare green tea noodles ahead of time, if desired. Combine matcha with flour, then add green tea infusion and egg yolks and mix into dough. Knead until dough is smooth. Allow dough to rest for about 1 hour. Using a pasta machine, roll dough out as thinly as possible, then cut into thin noodles (see Kitchen Techniques).

Prepare curry. Stir-fry red curry paste and curry powder with about 100 ml (3^1/$_2$ fl oz) coconut or soy milk until fragrant. Add remaining coconut or soy milk little by little and season with soy sauce and sugar.

Prepare beef. Season tenderloin with salt and pepper and place into a preheated sauté pan. Cook for 3 minutes on each side until medium rare. Set aside to rest for 5 minutes, then slice.

Meanwhile, heat oil and deep-fry green tea noodles until crisp. Set aside to drain well.

Divide fried noodles into individual serving bowls and top with sliced beef. Ladle curry into bowls. Garnish with crisp-fried shallots and coriander leaves. Serve with condiments on the side.

Jasmine-Chrysanthemum Tea Fettuccine with Mushrooms

Preparation Time: 45 minutes   Cooking Time: 10 minutes   Serves 4

FETTUCCINE

Water *100 ml (3¹/₂ fl oz)*

Jasmine tea leaves *5 g (¹/₆ oz)*

Chrysanthemum tea leaves *20 g (²/₃ oz)*

Plain flour *500 g (1 lb 1¹/₂ oz)*

Eggs *2*

Egg yolk *1*

Soy bean oil *as needed*

Salt or salt substitute *1¹/₂ tsp*

MUSHROOMS

Olive oil *for frying*

Enoki mushrooms *50 g (1²/₃ oz), base cut off*

Shiitake mushrooms *85 g (3 oz), caps wiped*

Button mushrooms *85 g (3 oz), caps wiped*

Salt or salt substitute *to taste*

Ground black pepper *to taste*

GARNISH

Spring onion *¹/₂, finely sliced*

Tomato *30 g (1 oz), cut into small cubes*

Prepare fettuccine. Bring water to a boil, then remove from heat. Add jasmine and chrysanthemum tea and leave to infuse for 5–10 minutes. Strain tea infusion into a mixing bowl, then add flour, eggs, egg yolk, 5 tsp soy bean oil and salt. Using an electric mixer fitted with a dough hook, knead until dough is formed. Continue to knead to smoothen dough, adding more flour if dough is too wet. Cover with a damp tea towel and set aside for about 1 hour. Roll rested dough out using a pasta machine and cut into thin strips (see Kitchen Techniques).

Bring a pot of water to a boil and cook fettuccine for 4–5 minutes or until al dente. Remove fettuccine immediately and strain, then toss with some soy bean oil so noodles do not stick.

Prepare mushrooms. Heat olive oil in a frying pan and sauté mushrooms lightly. Season to taste with salt and pepper. Toss mushrooms with fettuccine.

Garnish fettuccine with spring onion and tomato cubes. Serve immediately.

Photograph on pg 124–125

Cold Sesame Noodles with Ginseng Tea

Preparation Time: 45 minutes   Cooking Time: 10 minutes   Serves 4

GINSENG TEA INFUSION

Water *240 ml (8 fl oz / 1 cup)*

Ginseng tea *10 g (¹/₃ oz)*

Ginseng roots *60 g (2 oz)*

COLD SESAME NOODLES

Yellow wheat noodles *420 g (14 oz)*

Ginger *30 g (1 oz), peeled and grated*

Red chilli *15 g (¹/₂ oz), cut into fine strips*

Spring onions *120 g (4 oz), cut into fine strips*

Black sesame seeds *10 g (¹/₃ oz)*

Sesame oil *1 tsp*

Rice vinegar *1 Tbsp*

Salt or salt substitute *to taste*

Ground white pepper *to taste*

GARNISH

Finely shredded nori

Prepare ginseng tea infusion. Bring water to a boil in a small pot, then remove from heat. Add tea and ginseng roots and infuse for about 30 minutes. Refrigerate to chill, then strain before using.

Prepare cold sesame noodles. Cooking noodles in boiling water until just done, then drain and immediately plunge into iced water. Drain well, then place into chilled, strained ginseng tea infusion. Add all remaining ingredients, except garnish, to noodles and toss well. Adjust seasoning to taste.

Serve noodles cold. Garnished with shredded nori.

Photograph on pg 128–129

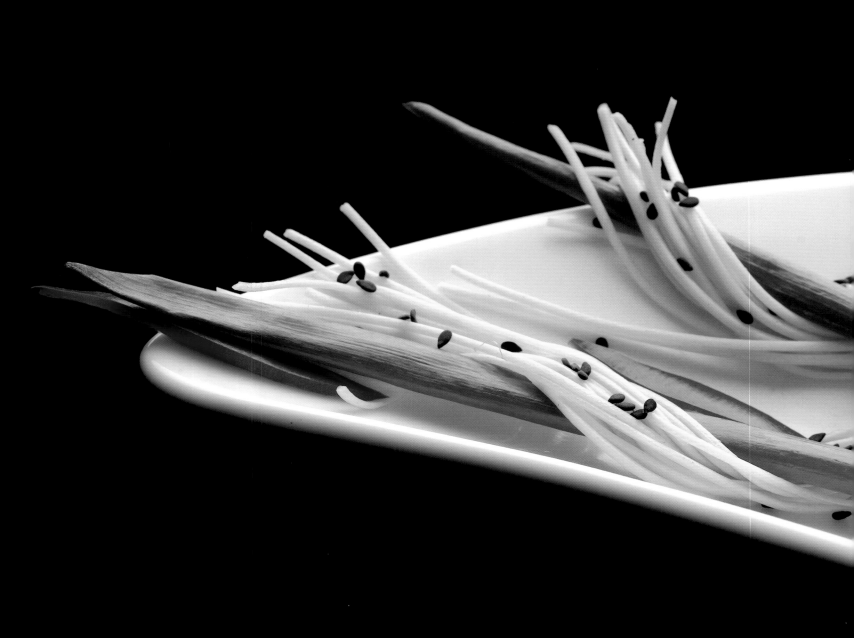

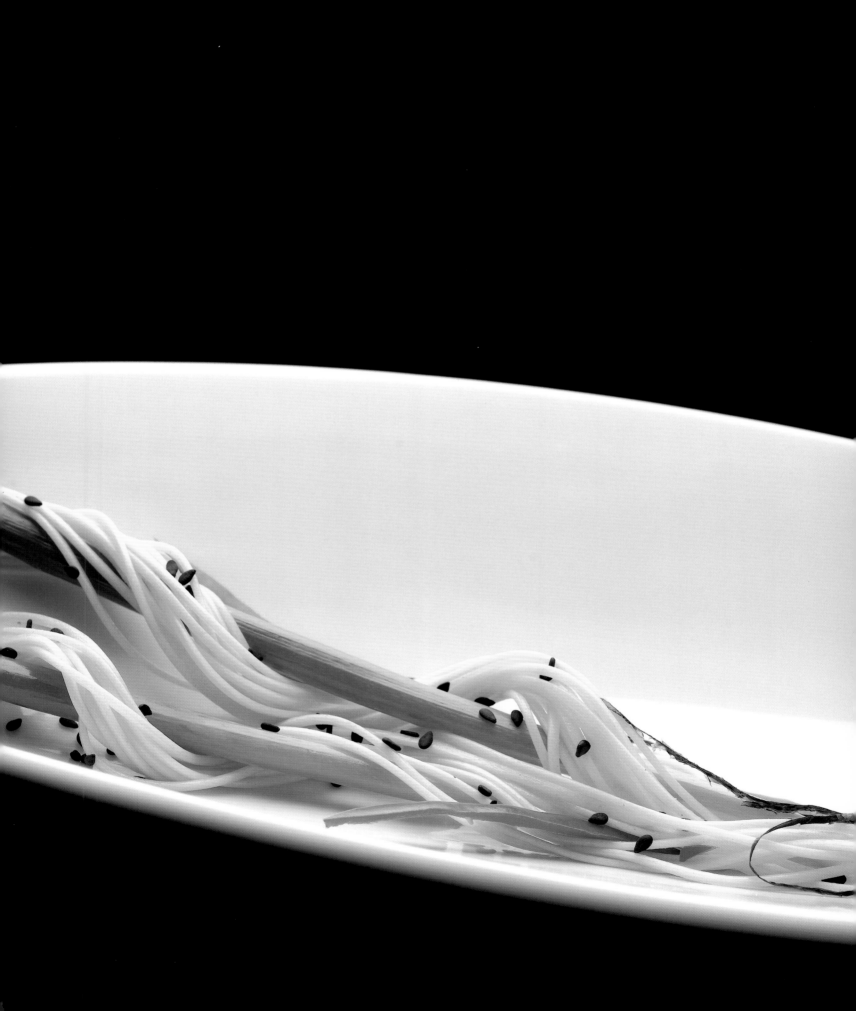

Jasmine Tea-Crusted Tuna Roll with Yam Noodles

Preparation Time: 20 minutes   Cooking Time: 1 hour   Serves 4

Yam noodles *200 g (7 oz), pre-cooked in chicken stock (see pg 178)*

TUNA ROLL

Nori sheets *2, cut in half*

Wasabi *50 g (1²/₃ oz)*

Tuna loin *4 pieces, each about 100 g (3¹/₂ oz)*

Jasmine tea leaves *30 g (1 oz), ground into a fine powder using a spice grinder*

SAUCE

Chicken stock (see pg 178) *400 ml (13 fl oz)*

Corn flour *30 g (1 oz)*

Light soy sauce *50 ml (1²/₃ fl oz)*

Shiitake mushrooms *75 g (2¹/₂ oz), stems removed and sliced*

Salt or salt substitute *to taste*

Ground white pepper *to taste*

TEMPURA BATTER

Ice *50 g (1²/₃ oz)*

Iced water *100 ml (3¹/₂ fl oz)*

Egg yolk *1*

Corn flour *75 g (2¹/₂ oz)*

Plain flour *50 g (1²/₃ oz)*

Canola oil *for deep-frying*

GARNISH

Finely shredded nori

Purple or green shiso leaves

Wasabi

Prepare tuna roll in advance. Brush nori sheets with wasabi. Coat tuna with jasmine tea leaves, then wrap in nori. Cover and refrigerate.

Prepare sauce. Bring chicken stock to a boil. Add a little water to corn flour to make a thick slurry. Stir slurry into stock while whisking continuously to thicken stock. Add soy sauce and mushrooms, then remove from heat. Season to taste with salt and pepper. Keep warm.

Prepare tempura batter. Combine ice, iced water and egg yolk, whisking thoroughly. Stir in corn flour and plain flour, but do not mix. Allow lumps to form. Set aside for 5 minutes. Heat canola oil to 180°C (350°F). Dust chilled tuna rolls with a little flour, then dip into tempura batter. Deep-fry coated rolls, one at a time, for 2–3 minutes, or to your preferred doneness (2 minutes for rare). Remove tuna and drain on paper towels.

Meanwhile, drain yam noodles and heat in warm sauce. Slice tuna into 1-cm (¹/₂-in) thick pieces.

Serve noodles with tuna, garnished with shredded nori, shiso leaves and wasabi, if desired.

Oolong Tea Linguini with Maine Lobster

Preparation Time: 2 hours   Cooking Time: 30 minutes   Serves 4

LINGUINI

Plain flour *240 g (8¹/₂ oz)*

Oolong tea *14 g (¹/₂ oz), ground into a fine powder using a spice grinder*

Egg yolks *6*

Egg *1*

Low-fat milk *1 Tbsp*

Olive oil *¹/₂ Tbsp*

LOBSTERS

Water *2 litres (64 fl oz / 8 cups)*

Shallots *40 g (1¹/₂ oz), peeled*

Lemon *1, cut in half*

Celery *55 g (2 oz)*

Thyme *2 sprigs*

Salt or salt substitute *to taste*

White peppercorns *to taste*

Maine lobsters *4, each about 675 g (1 lb 8 oz)*

SAUCE

Lobster stock (see pg 179) *2 litres (64 fl oz / 8 cups)*

Saffron threads *a pinch*

Light cream *60 ml (2 fl oz / 4 Tbsp)*

Salt or salt substitute *to taste*

BROAD BEANS

Water *1 litre (32 fl oz / 4 cups)*

Broad beans *100 g (3¹/₂ oz), removed from pods*

Salt or salt substitute *to taste*

Olive oil *60 ml (2 fl oz / 4 Tbsp)*

GARNISH (OPTIONAL)

Micro greens

Lobster coral

Prepare linguini. Place flour in a mixing bowl with ground oolong tea and create a well. Add egg yolks, egg, milk and olive oil to well, then gently bring flour over wet ingredients. Mix by hand in a circular motion until dough comes together. Knead dough for 10–15 minutes to create a smooth ball. Cover dough with plastic wrap and refrigerate for at least 30 minutes before using. Roll rested dough out using a pasta machine and cut into thin strips (see Kitchen Techniques).

Prepare lobsters. Place water in a large pot and add shallots, lemon, celery, thyme, salt and peppercorns. Bring to a boil and allow ingredients to cook for 5 minutes. Add whole lobsters and cook for 6–7 minutes. Remove lobsters and plunge into iced water. Once cool, remove claws and tails from bodies. Crack shells to remove meat (see Kitchen Techniques). Set lobster meat aside in the refrigerator until ready to use. Set aside lobster heads and shells for stock. Reserve lobster coral for use as garnish, if desired.

Prepare sauce. Reduce lobster stock in a large pot over medium heat to about 500 ml (16 fl oz / 2 cups). Skim impurities off surface as stock cooks. Once stock is reduced, add saffron, cream and salt. Set aside and keep hot.

Prepare broad beans. Bring water to a boil in a stockpot. Add broad beans and cook for 3 minutes, then drain beans and plunge immediately into iced water to chill. Remove beans from pods and toss with salt and olive oil.

When ready to serve, bring 2 litres (64 fl oz / 8 cups) water to a boil and cook linguini for 3–4 minutes or until al dente. Strain and toss with sauce.

Serve linguini with broad beans and lobster. Garnish with micro greens and lobster coral.

Green Tea Risotto with Roasted Pumpkin and Pepitas

Preparation Time: 30 minutes   Cooking Time: 30 minutes   Serves 4

PUMPKIN PURÉE

Vegetable oil *4 tsp*

Butternut pumpkin *100 g (3¹/₂ oz), peeled and chopped*

Marjoram *1 sprig*

Shallot *1, peeled and chopped*

Salt or salt substitute *to taste*

Ground black pepper *to taste*

Water *150 ml (5 fl oz)*

RISOTTO

Water *400 ml (13 fl oz)*

Green tea leaves *6 g (¹/₅ oz)*

Shallots *20 g (²/₃ oz), peeled and minced*

Butter or margarine *5 g (¹/₆ oz)*

Arborio, Vialone Nano or Carnaroli rice *90 g (3 oz)*

Salt or salt substitute *to taste*

PUMPKIN BALLS (OPTIONAL)

Butternut pumpkin *¹/₂, small*

Olive oil *1 Tbsp*

Butter or margarine *10 g (¹/₃ oz)*

Sugar or sugar substitute *30 g (1 oz)*

GARNISH

Toasted pepitas (pumpkin seeds)

Prepare pumpkin purée. Heat vegetable oil and sauté pumpkin, marjoram and shallot over medium heat for 2–3 minutes. Season to taste with salt and pepper. Add water and simmer until pumpkin is soft. Takes about 15 minutes. Place mixture in a blender and process until smooth. Strain through a sieve. Set aside.

Prepare pumpkin balls. Using a melon baller, scoop out balls of pumpkin. Blanch in lightly salted water for 3 minutes, then drain and sauté in olive oil until lightly brown. Add butter or margarine and sugar and cook until caramelized. Set aside and keep warm.

Prepare risotto about 20 minutes before serving. Heat water in a small pot to 70°C (155°F), then remove from heat. Add tea leaves, cover and steep for 5 minutes, then strain and discard leaves. Sauté shallots in butter or margarine over medium heat until translucent. Meanwhile, return infusion to heat and simmer. Add rice to shallots and stir well. Add pumpkin purée and a ladle of simmering green tea. Cook rice over low heat, stirring all the time. When liquid is absorbed, add some more green tea. Repeat until rice is tender yet still firm inside and creamy outside. Season to taste with salt.

Serve risotto with pumpkin balls. Garnish with toasted pepitas.

Soba Noodle Salad with Chipotle Chicken, Cocoa and Lapsang Souchong Tea

Preparation Time: 1 hour   Cooking Time: 30 minutes   Serves 4

NOODLE SALAD

Strong green tea infusion *1 litre (32 fl oz / 4 cups)*

Salt or salt substitute *a pinch*

Egg noodles *500 g (1 lb 1¹/₂ oz)*

Carrot *120 g (4¹/₂ oz), peeled and cut into fine strips*

Sugar snap peas *60 g (2 oz), cut into fine strips*

Cabbage *60 g (2 oz), cut into fine strips*

Red onion *60 g (2 oz), peeled and finely sliced*

Spring onions *2, cut into fine strips*

Orange *1, segmented*

DRESSING

Light soy sauce *60 ml (2 fl oz / 4 Tbsp)*

Rice wine vinegar *60 ml (2 fl oz / 4 Tbsp)*

Freshly squeezed orange juice *60 ml (2 fl oz / 4 Tbsp)*

Olive oil *60 ml (2 fl oz / 4 Tbsp)*

Sesame oil *60 ml (2 fl oz / 4 Tbsp)*

Peanuts *60 g (2 oz), finely chopped*

CHICKEN

Dried chipotle *30 g (1 oz), crushed*

Cocoa powder *30 g (1 oz)*

Lapsang Souchong tea leaves *30 g (1 oz)*

Salt or salt substitute *to taste*

Ground black pepper *to taste*

Chicken breasts *4, each about 180 g (6¹/₂ oz)*

Olive oil *for frying*

Prepare noodle salad. Place tea infusion in a large pot, add salt and bring to a boil. Add noodles and cook lightly. Drain noodles and place into iced water to cool. Reserve 60 ml (2 fl oz / 4 Tbsp) tea infusion for dressing. Drain noodles well and set aside.

Prepare dressing. Combine soy sauce, vinegar, reserved tea and orange juice in a mixing bowl. Slowly whisk in oils, then add peanuts. Set aside.

Prepare chicken. Preheat oven to 200°C (400°F). Combine chipotle, cocoa powder, tea leaves and salt and pepper. Dust chicken with this mixture. Heat oil in an ovenproof pan over high heat and sear chicken, then transfer to the oven and roast until chicken is cooked but still juicy. Takes about 10 minutes. Remove and set aside to cool. Slice chicken just before serving.

Toss noodles with carrot, sugar snap peas, cabbage, onion, spring onions and orange segments, then toss again with dressing.

Serve noodles with chicken. Garnish as desired.

Jasmine Tea Scented Red Rice with Langoustines

Start preparations 1 day ahead   Cooking Time: 30 minutes   Serves 4

RED RICE

Water *250 ml (8 fl oz / 4 cups)*

Jasmine tea *8 sachets*

Organic red rice *240 g (8¹/₂ oz), washed and drained*

Vegetable stock (see pg 179) *600 ml (20 fl oz / 2¹/₂ cups)*

Olive oil *1 Tbsp*

Onion *45 g (1¹/₂ oz), peeled and chopped*

Shiitake mushrooms *120 g (4¹/₂ oz), sliced*

White honshimeji mushrooms *120 g (4¹/₂ oz)*

Baby bok choy *4 stalks, blanched and cut in half*

Salt or salt substitute *to taste*

Ground white pepper *to taste*

LANGOUSTINES

Olive oil *1 Tbsp*

Langoustine tails (see Kitchen Techniques) *8, shelled and cleaned*

Salt or salt substitute *to taste*

Ground white pepper *to taste*

QUAIL EGGS

Olive oil *1 Tbsp*

Quail eggs (optional) *4*

GARNISH

Spring onions *4, cut into fine julienne and soaked in iced water*

Prepare red rice. Bring water to a boil, then remove from heat. Add tea sachets and steep for about 3 minutes. Remove and discard sachets. Combine red rice with vegetable stock and tea infusion, then steam for 20 minutes. Leave to cool completely, preferably overnight.

Heat olive oil in a pan and sauté onion and mushrooms until onion is translucent. Add rice and bok choy and sauté for another few seconds. Season to taste with salt and pepper and set aside.

Prepare langoustines. Heat olive oil in a clean pan and sear langoustine tails quickly. Season to taste with salt and pepper.

Prepare quail eggs. Heat another remaining olive oil in a clean pan and fry quail eggs "sunny side up".

Serve fried rice with langoustine tails and quail eggs. Garnish with spring onions.

Buckwheat Soba and Tuna Ribbons with Green Tea-Wasabi Dressing

Preparation Time: 45 minutes   Cooking Time: 10 minutes   Serves 4

Sushi-grade blue fin tuna *360 g (12 oz)*

EMULSION

Wasabi powder *15 g (1/2 oz)*

Matcha (green tea powder) *30 g (1 oz)*

Rice wine vinegar *2 Tbsp*

Champagne vinegar *2 Tbsp*

Canola oil *180 ml (6 fl oz / 3/4 cup)*

Salt or salt substitute *to taste*

Ground white pepper *to taste*

NOODLES

Water *2 litres (64 fl oz / 8 cups)*

Buckwheat soba noodles *200 g (7 oz)*

Sesame oil *2 Tbsp*

LOTUS ROOT CHIPS (OPTIONAL)

Lotus root *60 g (2 oz)*

Canola oil *1 litre (32 fl oz / 4 cups)*

Salt or salt substitute *to taste*

GARNISH (OPTIONAL)

Wasabi peas

Daikon sprouts

Prepare emulsion. Combine wasabi and green tea powders with both vinegars and stir until powders are dissolved. Slowly whisk in oil until dressing emulsifies and is thick. Season to taste with salt and pepper. This process can be done on low speed in a blender.

Slice tuna thinly, about 0.6-cm (1/4-in) thick, then slice again into ribbons.

Prepare noodles. Bring water to a boil, then add noodles, stirring to ensure that noodles do not stick. Cook until noodles soften but still have a bit of resistance when chewed. Takes about 3 minutes. Remove noodles and immediately plunge into iced water. Once noodles are cooled, drain and toss in sesame oil to prevent sticking.

Prepare lotus root chips. Cut lotus root into 0.2-cm (1/8-in) thin slices. Rinse in warm water for 15 minutes to wash off starch. Heat oil to 180°C. Remove lotus root slices from water and dry thoroughly. Drop lotus root slices into hot oil and fry until golden brown. Remove and season with salt. Set aside to drain well.

When ready to serve, toss soba with three-quarters of emulsion and season to taste with salt and pepper.

Serve soba with tuna ribbons. Garnish with lotus root chips, wasabi peas and daikon sprouts.

Desserts

Choosing a dessert can inspire two extremes in approach. There are diners who are stringent calorie counters, inclined towards the lean and spare. Others want to indulge and discount the calories for now. Here the Peninsula chefs have responded to both, coming up with desserts to satisfy all. Some chefs have turned to cream and milk, often infused with exotic tea flavours. Fruit, fruit and more fruit and fat-free yogurt inform the others in more spa-type delights. Be assured, however, that the healthy properties of tea — as well as those of herbal infusions such as rose hip, lemon verbena and raspberry leaf — make it into every recipe.

Raspberry Tea-Infused Rhubarb with Yogurt Sherbet

Start preparations 1 day ahead   Cooking Time: 20 minutes   Serves 4

RHUBARB

Water *150 ml (5 fl oz)*

Raspberry tea leaves *5 g (1/6 oz)*

Sugar or sugar substitute *50 g (1²/₃ oz)*

Lime *1, squeezed for juice*

Vanilla bean *¹/₂*

Raspberry purée *2 Tbsp*

Rhubarb *400 g (14¹/₃ oz), peeled and cut into 5-cm (2-in) lengths*

Grand Marnier *4 tsp*

Strawberries *8, hulled and cut in half*

YOGURT SHERBET

Water *45 ml (1¹/₂ fl oz / 3 Tbsp)*

Corn syrup *1 tsp*

Sugar or sugar substitute *45 g (1¹/₂ oz)*

Low-fat yogurt *140 g (5 oz)*

Fat-free sour cream *55 g (2 oz)*

Freshly squeezed lemon juice *2 tsp*

GARNISH (OPTIONAL)

Strawberries

Mint leaves

Prepare yogurt sherbet a day ahead. Bring water, corn syrup and sugar to a boil in a small pan. Place pan in an iced water bath until syrup is very cold. Gently mix in yogurt and sour cream. Add lemon juice and mix well. Churn in an ice cream machine according to the manufacturer's instructions. Freeze until set.

Prepare rhubarb. Heat water to 95°C (200°F) and pour over raspberry tea leaves placed in a saucepan. Allow to stand for 5 minutes, then strain infusion back into saucepan. Add sugar, lime juice, vanilla bean and raspberry purée. Bring to a boil, then add rhubarb and reduce heat to medium. Cook until rhubarb is tender. Takes about 10 minutes. Remove rhubarb from saucepan and set aside. Add Grand Marnier to saucepan and bring to a boil. Place saucepan in a big bowl of iced water to cool liquid down. Re-combine with rhubarb and set aside.

Serve lengths of rhubarb topped with yogurt sherbet on a plate, or dice rhubarb and serve with sauce in glasses, topped with yogurt sherbet. Garnish with strawberries and mint leaves.

White Chocolate Panna Cotta with Chai Tea

Preparation Time: 2 hours   Cooking Time: 45 minutes   Serves 4

PANNA COTTA

Gelatine sheets *4 leaves or 3 tsp gelatine powder*

Light cream *600 ml (20 fl oz / 2 1/2 cups)*

Cinnamon *2 sticks*

Cardamom pods *2, crushed*

Vanilla bean *1*

Ground white pepper *1/4 tsp*

Assam tea *3 sachets*

White chocolate *225 g (8 oz), chopped and melted*

Organic honey *for drizzling*

YOGURT CREAM

Light cream *120 ml (4 fl oz / 1/2 cup)*

Vanilla bean *1, split and seeds scraped out*

Plain non-fat yogurt *240 ml (8 fl oz / 1 cup)*

Sugar or sugar substitute *115 g (4 oz)*

COCOA NIB TUILE

Butter or margarine *65 g (2 1/2 oz)*

Sugar or sugar substitute *65 g (2 1/2 oz)*

Glucose or corn syrup *4 tsp*

Low-fat milk *4 tsp*

Cocoa nibs *25 g (1 oz)*

Ground almonds *105 g (3 1/2 oz)*

BALSAMIC REDUCTION

Balsamic vinegar *500 ml (16 fl oz / 2 cups)*

Freshly squeezed orange juice *120 ml (4 fl oz / 1/2 cup)*

Sugar or sugar substitute *115 g (4 oz)*

ORANGE CONFIT

Water *1 litre (32 fl oz / 4 cups)*

Sugar or sugar substitute *450 g (1 lb)*

Oranges *3, finely grated for zest*

GARNISH (OPTIONAL)

Chocolate strips

Prepare panna cotta. Soften gelatine sheets by soaking in just enough cold water to cover. Squeeze out excess water before using. If using gelatine powder, sprinkle over 60 ml (2 fl oz / 4 Tbsp) cold water and set aside. Bring cream, cinnamon, cardamom, vanilla and pepper to a boil in a saucepan. Remove from heat and add tea sachets. Leave to infuse for 30 minutes, then strain and return to a boil. Place gelatine and melted white chocolate in a mixing bowl, then pour tea infusion over and whisk until smooth. Strain again and pour into four 120-ml (4-fl oz / 1/2-cup) ramekins. Refrigerate until set. Takes about 2 hours.

Prepare yogurt cream. Place cream in a bowl with vanilla seeds, and whisk until mixture forms soft peaks. Add yogurt and sugar and whisk until stiff.

Prepare cocoa nib tuile. Place all ingredients except nibs and ground almonds into a saucepan and bring to a boil until sugar dissolves. Remove from heat and stir in nibs and ground almonds. Refrigerate to chill, then roll mixture out thinly on a silicone baking mat or greaseproof paper. Bake in a preheated oven at 190°C (370°F) for 10–12 minutes or until golden brown. Cut or break into pieces and set aside.

Prepare balsamic reduction. Place ingredients in a small saucepan and bring to a boil. Reduce until thick or until only a quarter of original liquid is left.

Prepare orange confit. Bring water and sugar to a boil in a saucepan, then add orange zest. Cook until orange zest is translucent, then strain syrup and keep at room temperature. Reserve some zest for decoration, if desired.

Unmould panna cotta and top with cocoa nib tuile and yogurt cream. Drizzle with balsamic reduction, orange confit and honey, then decorate with chocolate strips and reserved zest from orange confit.

Darjeeling Tea Dark Chocolate Mousse with Brownie

Preparation Time: 1 hour 30 minutes   Cooking Time: 30 minutes   Makes 4 medium-size tarts

CHOCOLATE MOUSSE

Low-fat milk *240 ml (8 fl oz / 1 cup)*

Darjeeling tea leaves *30 g (1 oz)*

Sugar or sugar substitute *120 g (4¹/₂ oz)*

Egg yolks *100 g (3¹/₂ oz)*

Gelatine sheets *2 leaves or 1¹/₂ tsp gelatine powder*

70% dark unsweetened chocolate *500 g (1 lb 1¹/₂ oz), chopped and melted*

Light cream *240 ml (8 fl oz / 1 cup)*

BROWNIE

Butter or margarine *250 g (9 oz)*

Sugar or sugar substitute *200 g (7 oz)*

Glucose or corn syrup *80 ml (2¹/₂ fl oz)*

Eggs *200 g (7 oz)*

Dark unsweetened chocolate *140 g (5 oz), chopped and melted*

Plain flour *100 g (3¹/₂ oz)*

Cocoa powder *20 g (²/₃ oz)*

Walnuts *100 g (3¹/₂ oz)*

Pecan nuts *100 g (3¹/₂ oz)*

CHOCOLATE SAUCE

Light cream *100 ml (3¹/₂ oz)*

70% dark unsweetened chocolate *100 g (3¹/₂ oz), chopped*

Glucose or corn syrup *2 tsp*

Prepare chocolate mousse. Bring milk to a boil in a saucepan. Remove from heat and add tea leaves. Leave to infuse for 5–10 minutes, then strain and return infusion to saucepan and bring to a boil. Meanwhile, whip together sugar and egg yolks until pale or lemon-coloured. Turn beaters to slow and add milk 3 intervals, beating constantly until well incorporated each time. Place mixture in a saucepan and cook over medium heat, stirring until mixture thickens. Temperature should read 85°C (185°F) on a candy thermometer. Cool to 35°C (95°F).

Meanwhile, soften gelatine by soaking in just enough cold water to cover sheets. Squeeze out excess water before using. If using powdered gelatine, sprinkle over 2 Tbsp cold water until dissolved. Add gelatine to melted chocolate and stir for 2 minutes. Add to egg and milk mixture and mix well.

Whip cream to medium-stiff peaks. Fold into chocolate mixture with a rubber spatula.

Prepare brownie. Preheat oven to 180°C (350°F). Grease a 23-cm (9-in) square baking tin and set aside. Combine butter or margarine, sugar and glucose or corn syrup in a mixing bowl, then add eggs a little at a time, until well incorporated. Add melted chocolate, then flour, cocoa powder and nuts. Pour into prepared tin and bake for 15 minutes. Remove from oven and allow to cool.

Prepare chocolate sauce. Heat cream and add chocolate, stirring until chocolate is dissolved. Add glucose or corn syrup. Set aside.

To assemble brownies, select a ring cutter with the same circumference as the mould for mousse and grease sides with butter. Cut out brownies and set aside. Pour mousse into moulds, filling it up to two-thirds. Place in freezer for 5–10 minutes, then add pre-cut brownies. Freeze for a few hours. To unmould, run a knife around the inside rim of moulds, or run hot water on the outside for a few seconds.

Alternatively, cut brownie into squares and set mousse into a loaf-shaped mould, or paté mould lined with plastic wrap. Place in freezer for a few hours, then cut out squares of mousse.

Serve brownies and mousse with vanilla ice cream (see pg 152) and drizzle with chocolate sauce.

Chamomile Tea Panna Cotta with Lemon Sorbet and Berry Sauce

Start preparations 1 day ahead   Cooking Time: 20 minutes   Serves 4

LEMON SORBET

Water *250 ml (8 fl oz / 4 cups)*

Sugar or sugar substitute *220 g (8 oz)*

Freshly squeezed lemon juice *250 ml (8 fl oz / 4 cups)*

Lemon *1, grated for zest*

PANNA COTTA

Chamomile tea flowers *5 g (¹/₆ oz)*

Low-fat milk *500 ml (16 fl oz / 2 cups)*

Gelatine sheets *4 leaves or 3 tsp gelatine powder*

Low-fat cream *500 ml (16 fl oz / 2 cups)*

Sugar or sugar substitute *220 g (8 oz)*

Lemon *1, grated for zest*

Orange *¹/₂, grated for zest*

BERRY SAUCE

Raspberries *275 g (10 oz)*

Lemon *1, grated for zest and squeezed for 2 Tbsp juice*

Sugar or sugar substitute *to taste*

Agar powder (optional) *¹/₈ tsp*

GARNISH

Mixed berries

Hearts on fire or mint leaves

NOTE
This recipe is simple to make when the sorbet and panna cotta are prepared one day in advance.

Prepare sorbet. Bring water and sugar to a boil in a small saucepan. Remove from heat and set aside to cool. Stir in lemon juice and zest. Churn using an ice cream machine according to manufacturer's instructions. Freeze to set.

Prepare panna cotta. Place tea in milk and refrigerate overnight. Soften gelatine by soaking in just enough cold water to cover sheets. Squeeze out excess water before using. If using powdered gelatine, sprinkle over 60 ml (2 fl oz / 4 Tbsp) cold water and set aside. Bring all panna cotta ingredients (including infused milk,) except gelatine, to a simmer. Remove from heat and allow to stand for about 15 minutes, then strain and add gelatine, stirring until gelatine is fully dissolved. Pour mixture into 4 ramekins and refrigerate for 2 hours.

Prepare berry sauce. Purée half of raspberries and strain using a fine sieve. Add zest and juice to strained purée, then fold in remaining whole raspberries. Add sugar to taste. Berry sauce can be poured over panna cotta or set into a 0.5-cm (¹/₄-in) thick layer using ¹/₈ tsp agar powder. Cut out rounds of berry sauce agar using a ring cutter of a size similar to that of ramekins.

Unmould panna cotta and spoon berry sauce or place berry sauce agar over. Garnish with mixed berries, hearts on fire or mint leaves.

Vanilla Ice Cream with Sencha Crumble and Kumquat Compote

Preparation Time: 4 hours   Cooking Time: 30 minutes   Serves 4

SENCHA JELLY

Mineral water *300 ml (10 fl oz / 1¼ cups)*

Sencha powder *20 g (²/₃ oz)*

Agar powder *10 g (¹/₃ oz)*

Sugar or sugar substitute *45 g (1¹/₂ oz)*

SENCHA CRUMBLE

Butter or margarine *60 g (2 oz)*

Sugar or sugar substitute *60 g (2 oz)*

Cake flour *60 g (2 oz)*

Almond powder *45 g (1¹/₂ oz)*

Sencha powder *10 g (¹/₃ oz)*

Icing sugar *10 g (¹/₃ oz)*

VANILLA ICE CREAM

Low-fat milk *210 ml (7 fl oz)*

Light cream *210 ml (7 fl oz)*

Vanilla bean *1, split*

Sugar or sugar substitute *90 g (3 oz)*

Egg yolks *1¹/₂*

KUMQUAT COMPOTE

Mineral water *240 ml (8 fl oz / 1 cup)*

Kumquats *150 g (5¹/₃ oz), cut in half*

Sugar or sugar substitute *150 g (5¹/₃ oz)*

Prepare jelly. Bring mineral water to a boil and let it cool to 80°C (176°F). Add tea powder and set aside for 3 minutes. Strain and stir in agar and sugar. Place into a shallow pan and leave to set at room temperature.

Prepare crumble. Preheat oven to 160°C (325°F). In a bowl, stir together butter or margarine, sugar, flour, almond powder and half the tea powder. Spread mixture onto a baking sheet. You may use a silicone mat to make it easier to remove after baking. Bake for 15 minutes, then remove from oven. Combine remaining tea powder with icing sugar and sprinkle on top of crumble while still warm. Break or cut into 4 equal pieces.

Prepare vanilla ice cream. Place milk, cream and vanilla bean in a deep saucepan over high heat and bring to a boil. Using an electric mixer, beat sugar and egg yolks until lemon-coloured. While beating, slowly add milk-cream mixture until well incorporated. Return mixture to saucepan and cook over low heat until 80°C (176°F), stirring constantly. Remove from heat and put saucepan into iced water to cool mixture. Pour cooled mixture into an ice cream machine and churn according to manufacturer's instructions. Freeze until set (see Kitchen Techniques).

Prepare kumquat compote. Bring 2 pots of water to the boil. Place kumquats into one pot and boil for 2 minutes, then remove and place into second pot of boiling water. Cook for another 2 minutes, then drain and discard water. Heat mineral water over medium heat, then add sugar and stir until sugar dissolves and syrup is thick. Add blanched kumquats and remove from heat.

Cut jelly into small shapes and serve with crumble, ice cream and kumquat compote.

Medjool Date Beignets with Orange Sabayon and Earl Grey Tea

Start preparations 1 day ahead   Cooking Time: 30 minutes   Serves 4

DATES

Water *500 ml (16 fl oz / 2 cups)*

Earl Grey tea leaves *10 g (¹/₃ oz)*

Sugar or sugar substitute *50 g (1²/₃ oz)*

Ginger *10 g (¹/₃ oz), peeled and sliced*

Star anise *2*

Cinnamon stick *1*

Vanilla bean *1, split*

Organic Medjool dates *200 g (7 oz)*

Marzipan (almond paste) *80 g (3 oz)*

Vegetable oil *for deep-frying*

ORANGE SABAYON

Gelatine sheet *1 leaf or ³/₄ tsp gelatine powder*

Freshly squeezed orange juice *250 ml (8 fl oz / 4 cups)*

Vanilla bean *¹/₄*

Egg yolk *1*

Sugar or sugar substitute *30 g (1 oz)*

Light whipping cream *150 ml (5 fl oz), whipped*

TEMPURA BATTER

Plain flour *2 cups*

Corn flour *1 cup*

Salt *¹/₂ tsp*

Baking powder *2 tsp*

Iced water *500 ml (16 fl oz / 2 cups)*

EARL GREY TEA

Earl Grey tea leaves *3 Tbsp, ground into a fine powder using a spice grinder*

Icing sugar *3 Tbsp*

Ground black pepper *1 Tbsp*

Prepare dates 1 day ahead. Heat water to 95°C (200°F) and pour over Earl Grey tea leaves. Leave to infuse for 5 minutes, then strain and discard tea leaves. Place sugar in a small, dry, heavy saucepan over medium-high heat. (A spoonful of water may be added to help dissolve sugar.) The sugar will begin to melt and turn light brown. Add ginger, star anise, cinnamon and vanilla bean. Add Earl Grey tea infusion and bring to a boil for 1 minute or until caramelized sugar is dissolved. Remove from heat and let mixture cool to room temperature. Cut dates lengthwise and remove seeds. Soak overnight in tea mixture. Remove dates from tea, pat dry and stuff with marzipan.

Prepare orange sabayon. Soak gelatine sheets in cold water to cover for 5–6 minutes. Squeeze out excess water before use. Alternatively, dissolve gelatine powder in 1 Tbsp cold water. Bring orange juice to a boil and add vanilla bean. Lower heat and simmer until reduced by half and strain. Using an electric mixer, beat egg yolk and sugar until pale or lemon-coloured. Turn mixer speed to low and stir in orange juice mixture. Place bowl of orange-egg yolk mixture over a pan of simmering water, whisking constantly until mixture thickens, about 10 minutes. Add gelatine and stir until thoroughly dissolved. Fold in whipped cream.

Prepare tempura. Combine dry ingredients, then add iced water to achieve a smooth batter. Set aside for 5 minutes. Heat oil to 185°C (365°F). Dredge dates in tempura batter and drop carefully into hot oil. Remove as soon as batter is lightly coloured. Drain on paper towels.

Prepare Earl Grey tea. Combine ground Earl Grey tea leaves, icing sugar and pepper and mix well.

Serve beignets with sabayon and Earl Grey powder. Garnish as desired.

Tea-Braised Rhubarb with Oishi Plum Sorbet and Rose Hip Syrup

Start preparations 2 hours ahead   Cooking Time: 20 minutes   Serves 4

ROSE HIP SYRUP

Mineral water *300 ml (10 fl oz / 1¹/₄ cups)*

Rose hip tea *10 g (¹/₃ oz)*

Sugar or sugar substitute *50 g (1²/₃ oz)*

Agar powder *3 g (¹/₁₀ oz)*

PLUM SORBET

Oishi plums or sweet plums *500 g
    (1 lb 1¹/₂ oz)*

Sugar or sugar substitute *90 g (3 oz)*

Mineral water *60 ml (2 fl oz / 4 Tbsp)*

RHUBARB

Rose hip tea *5 g (¹/₆ oz)*

Sugar or sugar substitute *90 g (3 oz)*

Rhubarb *180 g (6¹/₂ oz), peeled and cut into
    5-cm (2-in) lengths*

Grenadine syrup *45 ml (1¹/₂ fl oz / 4 Tbsp)*

GARNISH (OPTIONAL)

Fresh mixed fruit

Prepare rose hip syrup. Bring water to a boil in a small saucepan, then remove from heat. Add tea and leave to infuse for 10 minutes. Strain through filter paper back into pan. In a bowl, combine sugar with agar powder. Add rose hip infusion and stir until sugar is dissolved.

Prepare plum sorbet. Peel and remove pits from plums, then purée in a blender with sugar and water. Place mixture into an ice cream machine and churn according to manufacturer's instructions. Freeze until needed.

Prepare rhubarb. Sprinkle tea and sugar over rhubarb and allow to stand for 2 hours. Place rhubarb on a baking tray and pour grenadine syrup over. Cover with aluminium foil and bake at 160°C (325°F) for about 15 minutes.

Serve rhubarb with sorbet and rose hip syrup. Garnish with fresh mixed fruit.

Chocolate Tart with Oolong Tea Sherbet

Preparation Time: 2 hours   Cooking Time: 15 minutes   Serves 4

TART SHELLS

Butter or margarine *150 g (5^1/$_3$ oz)*

Icing sugar *45 g (1^1/$_2$ oz)*

Plain flour *150 g (5^1/$_3$ oz)*

Cocoa powder *25 g (1 oz)*

Ground almonds *55 g (2 oz)*

CHOCOLATE FILLING

Low-fat milk *50 ml (1^2/$_3$ fl oz)*

Oolong tea leaves *15 g (^{1}/$_2$ oz)*

Semi-sweet chocolate *50 g (1^2/$_3$ oz), chopped*

Dark unsweetened chocolate *50 g (1^2/$_3$ oz), chopped*

Butter or margarine *15 g (^{1}/$_2$ oz)*

OOLONG TEA SHERBET

Low-fat milk *250 ml (8 fl oz / 1 cup)*

Brown sugar *50 g (1^2/$_3$ oz)*

Oolong tea leaves *2 g (^{1}/$_{15}$ oz)*

NOTE
To blind bake means to partially cook the pie crust before the filling is added. Dried beans or pie weights are placed on the dough to keep it from rising (and weakening the crust) while baking.

Prepare tart shells. Combine butter or margarine and icing sugar until well blended. Set aside. Combine flour, cocoa powder and ground almonds, then stir into butter or margarine mixture to form dough. Shape dough into a disk, then cover with plastic wrap and refrigerate for 10–20 minutes.

Preheat oven to 170°C (330°F). Roll out dough and line four 10–12-cm (4–5-in) tart moulds with dough. Blind bake for 10–12 minutes, then remove from oven. Leave to cool before removing from moulds.

Prepare chocolate filling. Bring milk to a boil in a saucepan, then remove from heat and add tea leaves. Set aside to infuse for 10 minutes. Strain milk back into saucepan, then bring to a near-boil. Remove from heat and stir in chocolate and butter or margarine until mixture is smooth. Cool to room temperature. Fill tart shells and refrigerate for 30 minutes.

Prepare oolong tea sherbet. Place milk and brown sugar in a saucepan and bring to a boil. Add tea leaves and set aside for 10 minutes. Strain and churn in an ice cream machine according to manufacturer's instructions. Freeze until set.

Serve tarts with sherbet. Garnish with chocolate.

Earl Grey Infused Banana Glacé with Coffee Crumb
Start preparations 4 hours ahead   Cooking Time: 45 minutes   Serves 4

CANDIED WALNUTS

Sugar or sugar substitute *200 g (7 oz)*

Butter or margarine *85 g (3 oz)*

Walnuts *220 g (8 oz), toasted*

COFFEE CRUMB (OPTIONAL)

Sugar or sugar substitute *250 g (9 oz)*

Almond flour *250 g (9 oz)*

Plain flour *150 g (1²/₃ oz)*

Cocoa powder *60 g (2 oz)*

Ground coffee *50 g (1²/₃ oz)*

Butter or margarine *200 g (7 oz), melted*

Kosher salt *20 g (²/₃ oz)*

BANANA CHIPS (OPTIONAL)

Banana *1*

Simple syrup **(see pg 167)** *for brushing*

BANANA GLACÉ

Sugar or sugar substitute *170 g (6 oz)*

Egg yolks *4*

Bananas *2*

Mascarpone cheese *250 ml (8 fl oz / 1 cup)*

Light whipping cream *500 ml (16 fl oz / 2 cups), whipped to soft peaks*

Earl Grey tea leaves *10 g (¹/₃ oz), ground into a fine powder using a spice grinder*

GARNISH (OPTIONAL)

Chocolate pieces

Icing sugar

NOTE
Candied walnuts, coffee crumb and banana chips can be prepared ahead of time.

Prepare candied walnuts. Using a candy thermometer, cook sugar in a heavy-based pan to 120°–130°C (250°–260°F). Use a spoonful of water in sugar, if desired. Add butter or margarine and stir to combine. Add walnuts and stir to coat with caramel. Spread mixture on a silicone mat to cool, then chop into small pieces.

Prepare coffee crumb. Combine all ingredients for coffee crumb until sandy in texture. Make darker by using cocoa powder with a higher cocoa content and vice versa. Set aside.

Prepare banana chips. Preheat oven to 110°C (230°F). Peel and slice banana as thinly as possible, then dip slices into simple syrup. Place on a silicone baking sheet and bake for 30–40 minutes. Set aside to cool.

Prepare banana glacé. Using a candy thermometer, cook sugar in a small saucepan to 118°C (245°F), or until the soft-ball stage. It will look like a light caramel syrup. (A small spoonful of water may be added for easier mixing.) With an electric mixer, beat egg yolks. While beating, add caramel slowly in a thin stream. Continue to beat until mixture cools to room temperature. Purée bananas and add mascarpone cheese. Beat until smooth, then gently fold into cooled egg yolk mixture. Fold in whipped cream and candied walnuts. Stir in Earl Grey tea powder. Spoon mixture into four 8-cm (3-in) dessert rings placed on trays or into any freezer container. Freeze for at least 4 hours until set.

Unmould banana glacé or cut into fun shapes and place onto coffee crumb. Garnish with banana chips and chocolate pieces. Dust with icing sugar.

Warm Peach and Almond Cake with Raspberry Tea Sorbet

Preparation Time: 2 hours   Cooking Time: 30 minutes   Serves 4

PEACH AND ALMOND CAKE

Unsalted butter *150 g (5¹/₃ oz)*

Fructose sugar *150 g (5¹/₃ oz)*

Ground almonds *150 g (5¹/₃ oz)*

Peach tea leaves *3 g (¹/₁₀ oz), ground*

Eggs *3, lightly whisked*

Peaches *2, peeled and cut into pieces*

Organic honey *85 g (3 oz)*

RASPBERRY TEA SORBET

Gelatine sheets *2 leaves or 1¹/₂ tsp gelatine powder*

Water *550 ml (18 fl oz)*

Raspberry tea leaves *40 g (1¹/₂ oz)*

Fructose sugar *85 g (3 oz)*

Glucose or corn syrup *50 ml (1²/₃ fl oz)*

Raspberry purée *85 ml (2¹/₂ fl oz / ¹/₃ cup)*

GARNISH (OPTIONAL)

Green tea shortbread with black sesame seeds

Honey and blood orange jelly

Prepare peach and almond cake. Preheat oven to 160°C (325°F). Butter four round cake tins, each about 8-cm (3-in) in diameter, or 4–5 pastry rings, each about 7.5-cm (3-in) tall and 5-cm (2-in) wide. If using pastry rings, cover one side with foil. Set aside. Melt butter and add fructose sugar, ground almonds and ground tea. Whisk in eggs until well combined, then fold in peaches. Spoon mixture evenly into prepared tins or rings. Bake for 17–20 minutes. Leave cakes in tins for 5 minutes before removing. Brush with honey.

Prepare raspberry tea sorbet. Soften gelatine by soaking in just enough cold water to cover sheets. Squeeze out excess water before using. If using powdered gelatine, sprinkle over 2 Tbsp cold water and set aside. Bring water to a boil in a saucepan and add raspberry tea. Remove from heat and leave to infuse for 10 minutes. Strain infusion back into saucepan, then return to a boil. Stir in fructose sugar, glucose or corn syrup, gelatine and raspberry purée. Allow to cool before churning in an ice cream machine according to manufacturer's instructions. Freeze until set.

Serve cakes warm with raspberry tea sorbet. Garnish with shortbread and jelly.

Chilled Silken Tofu with Red Dates in Pu'er Tea

Start preparations 8 hours ahead   Cooking Time: 20 minutes   Serves 4

Silken tofu *200 g (7 oz)*

Water *950 ml (31¹/₂ fl oz)*

Pu'er tea leaves *25 g (1 oz)*

Sugar or sugar substitute *25 g (1 oz)*

Salt or salt substitute *12 g (²/₅ oz)*

Seedless red dates (see Glossary) *10*

NOTE

As an alternative to the silken tofu used this recipe, use tofu jelly (known as *dohua* in Chinese). Tofu jelly is even more delicate than silken tofu, and must be scooped by the spoonful into the stock.

Prepare tea stock. Bring water to a boil, then lower heat and add tea leaves, sugar, salt and red dates. Simmer over low heat for 15 minutes or until dates are very tender.

Cut tofu into cubes or balls using a melon baller and place into tea stock. Cover and refrigerate for 8 hours or overnight.

Serve chilled tofu in tea infusion.

Genmai Cha Soufflé and Champagne Float with Cinnamon Sorbet

Start preparations 4 hours ahead   Cooking Time: 15 minutes   Serves 4

GINGER SUGAR

Ginger *20 g (²/3 oz), peeled and grated*

Sugar or sugar substitute *110 g (4 oz)*

PASTRY CREAM (MAKES 750 G / 25 OZ)

Whole milk *500 ml (16 fl oz / 2 cups)*

Granulated sugar *125 g (4¹/2 oz)*

Plain flour *35 g (1 oz)*

Egg yolks *120 g (4¹/2 oz)*

Vanilla extract *1 tsp*

Butter *50 g (1²/3 oz)*

SIMPLE SYRUP

Water *750 ml (24 fl oz / 3 cups)*

Sugar or sugar substitute *700 g (1¹/2 lb)*

CINNAMON SORBET AND CHAMPAGNE FLOAT

Water *60 ml (2 fl oz / 4 Tbsp)*

Ceylon cinnamon *3 sticks*

Cassia *3 sticks*

Strawberry purée *375 g (12¹/2 oz)*

Champagne *750 ml (24 fl oz / 3 cups), chilled*

SOUFFLÉ

Butter or margarine *30 g (1 oz), softened*

Uncooked rice *30 g (1 oz)*

Ginger sugar *30 g (1 oz)*

Pastry cream (recipe below) *65 g (2¹/2 oz)*

Genmai cha (see Glossary) *5 g (¹/6 oz), ground into a fine powder using a spice grinder*

Egg whites *165 g (6 oz)*

Sugar or sugar substitute *35 g (1 oz)*

Freshly squeezed lemon juice *1 tsp*

Prepare ginger sugar. Combine ginger and sugar and mix well. This recipe only requires 30 g (1 oz) ginger sugar. Store excess in the refrigerator for future use.

Prepare pastry cream. Bring milk and half the sugar to a boil in a medium saucepan over high heat. Set aside. Whisk remaining sugar, plain flour and egg yolks until combined, then slowly whisk in half of the hot milk a little at a time. Return mixture to saucepan with remaining milk, whisking to combine. Stir mixture continuously over medium heat and return to a slow boil. Mixture will start to thicken and coat the back of a wooden spoon. Remove from heat and place in shallow heatproof plastic container. Pastry cream will keep for up to 7 days in the refrigerator. This recipe requires only 65 g (2¹/2 oz) pastry cream.

Preheat oven to 200°C (400°F). Toast rice in oven until golden, then cool completely and grind in a spice mill. Sift together with ginger sugar and set aside.

Prepare simple syrup. Bring water to a boil and add sugar. Heat, stirring occasionally. until sugar is dissolved. Refrigerate excess syrup for later use.

Prepare cinnamon sorbet. Bring 300 ml (10 fl oz / 1¹/4 cups) simple syrup, water and cinnamon and cassia sticks in a saucepan to a simmer. Remove from heat and cover with plastic wrap. Let infuse for 20 minutes, then remove cinnamon and cassia sticks. Stir in strawberry purée, then strain and pour into an ice cream machine. Churn according to manufacturer's instructions. When done, remove to a plastic container and freeze for at least 4 hours before serving.

Prepare champagne float. Place 4 serving glasses in the freezer at least 30 minutes before serving. About 5 minutes before soufflé is removed from oven, remove glasses from freezer. With a small melon baller, spoon 1–3 balls of cinnamon sorbet into each glass and pour chilled champagne over.

Prepare soufflé (see Kitchen Techniques). Preheat oven to 190°C (370°F). Soufflé is ready when risen above rim of ramekin and slightly browned. Takes 7–8 minutes.

Serve soufflé immediately with champagne float.

Beverages

Tea is a natural fit when it comes to the mixed drinks we like to imbibe, refreshing and giving "oomph" between meals. In the following recipes Peninsula chefs have chosen well-known teas such as green tea and Earl Grey, as well as the more unusual mango and black currant tea as the bases for certain fusions. Fruity tea flavours complement those fruits blended into smoothies. A herbal mint tea is combined with ginger juice and lemongrass — all healing ingredients — to make a bracing non-alcoholic cocktail. These healing beverages take just a few minutes to make. Put them together with ease. And enjoy.

Peach Smoothie with Black Currant Tea

Start preparations 1 hour ahead   Serves 4

Peaches 6

Water 350 ml (11²/₃ fl oz)

Black currant tea leaves 30 g (1 oz)

Organic honey or sugar substitute 55 g (2 oz)

Plain non-fat yogurt 110 g (4 oz)

Peel and slice peaches. Discard pit and freeze for 1 hour.

Bring water to a boil, then remove from heat. Add tea and leave to infuse for about 8 minutes before straining. Refrigerate infusion.

Blend frozen peaches, honey, yogurt and chilled tea for 45 seconds or until smooth. Pour into chilled glasses and serve immediately.

Japanese Green Tea Smoothie

Preparation Time: 15 minutes   Serves 4

Skimmed milk 300 ml (10 fl oz / 1¼ cups)

Plain non-fat yogurt 2 Tbsp

Matcha (green tea powder) 40 g (1¹/₂ oz)

Wildflower honey or sugar substitute 10 g (¹/₃ oz) or to taste

Ice 500 g (1 lb 1¹/₂ oz)

Combine all ingredients in a blender and blend until smooth. Pour into chilled glasses and serve immediately.

Mixed Berry Smoothie

Preparation Time: 15 minutes   Serves 4

Water 250 ml (8 fl oz / 1 cup)

Black cherry or white orchard tea leaves 10 g (¹/₃ oz)

Raspberries 550 g (18¹/₃ oz)

Strawberries 400 g (14¹/₃ oz)

Organic honey or sugar substitute 3 Tbsp

Plain non-fat yogurt 250 ml (8 fl oz / 1 cup)

Ice 500 g (1 lb 1¹/₂ oz)

Bring water to a boil, then remove from heat. Add tea and leave to infuse for about 8 minutes before straining. Refrigerate infusion.

Combine tea infusion, berries, honey or sugar and yogurt in a blender and blend until smooth. Add ice and blend again. Pour into chilled glasses and serve immediately.

Photograph on pg 171. Yellow glass: Peach Smoothie with Black Currant Tea; Green glass: Japanese Green Tea Smoothie; Pink glass: Mixed Berry Smoothie

Earl Grey Iced Tea with Ginger and Pineapple

Preparation Time: 40 minutes   Serves 4

Strong Earl Grey tea infusion *500 ml (16 fl oz / 2 cups)*

Freshly squeezed pineapple juice *500 ml (16 fl oz / 2 cups)*

Ginger *30 g (1 oz), peeled and sliced*

Honey or sugar substitute *2 Tbsp*

Crushed ice *450 g (1 lb)*

Strain tea infusion and refrigerate to chill.

Blend chilled tea infusion, pineapple juice, ginger, honey and crushed ice until smooth. Pour into chilled glasses. Decorate as desired and serve immediately.

Tropical Fruit Iced Tea

Preparation Time: 45 minutes   Serves 4

Yuzu juice *2 Tbsp*

Orange tea infusion *300 ml (10 fl oz / 1¹/₄ cups)*

Crushed ice *450 g (1 lb)*

FRUITS

Pineapple *60 g (2 oz)*

Kiwi *60 g (2 oz)*

Mandarin orange *60 g (2 oz)*

Mango *60 g (2 oz)*

Passion fruit *60 g (2 oz)*

Lychee *60 g (2 oz)*

Remove skin and seeds from fruits. Cut fruits into cubes. Blend fruits with yuzu juice, tea infusion and crushed ice until smooth. Pour into chilled glasses. Decorate as desired and serve immediately.

Mint Tea Cocktail

Preparation Time: 5 minutes   Serves 4

Water *840 ml (28 fl oz)*

Lemongrass (see Glossary) *30 g (1 oz), ends trimmed, hard outer leaves removed*

Ginger *100 g (3¹/₂ oz), peeled*

Sugar or sugar substitute *60 g (2 oz)*

Mint tea infusion *320 ml (10²/₃ fl oz)*

Crushed ice *450 g (1 lb)*

GARNISH (OPTIONAL)

Mint leaves, finely sliced

Bring 240 ml (8 fl oz / 1 cup) water to a boil and simmer lemongrass until water is reduced to about 160 ml (5¹/₃ fl oz). Strain and refrigerate to chill. Bring another 240 ml (8 floz / 1 cup) water to a boil and simmer ginger until water is reduced by half. Strain and refrigerate to chill.

Boil remaining water and sugar until sugar is dissolved. Cool syrup to room temperature.

Combine lemongrass juice, ginger juice, mint tea infusion and syrup and stir to mix well. Pour into chilled glasses. Decorate with finely sliced mint leaves and serve immediately.

Photograph on pg 172. Clockwise from top left: Earl Grey Iced Tea with Ginger and Pineapple; Mint Tea Cocktail; Tropical Fruit Iced Tea

Oolong Apple Cider with Apple Beignet

Start preparations 2 hours ahead Cooking Time: 20 minutes Serves 4

BEIGNET

Sugar or sugar substitute *210 g (7 oz)*

Salt or salt substitute *25 g (1 oz)*

Powdered non-fat milk *75 g (2¹/₂ oz)*

Bread flour *1.5 kg (3 lb 4¹/₂ oz)*

Fresh yeast *75 g (2¹/₂ oz)*

Vegetable shortening *150 g (5¹/₃ oz)*

Eggs *4*

Water *820 ml (27¹/₃ fl oz)*

Apples *2, peeled and cut into 1.5-cm (³/₄-in) dice*

Canola oil *for deep-frying*

OOLONG APPLE CIDER

Fresh apple cider *1 litre (32 fl oz / 4 cups)*

Orange *¹/₂, grated for zest*

Cinnamon *1 stick*

Cloves *2*

Oolong tea leaves *6 g (¹/₅ oz)*

CINNAMON SUGAR

Ground cinnamon *20 g (²/₃ oz)*

Castor sugar or sugar substitute *100 g (3¹/₂ oz)*

Prepare oolong apple cider. Place cider, orange zest and spices into a medium saucepan. Bring to a simmer, then reduce heat and cook for 10 minutes. Remove from heat and add tea leaves. Let steep for 4 minutes, then strain.

Prepare beignet. Combine sugar, salt, powdered milk and bread flour in a mixing bowl. Crumble yeast on top. Add shortening, eggs, water and apples. With a dough hook attachment, combine ingredients until dough starts to form and is kneaded. Takes 5–7 minutes. Remove dough onto a floured work surface, then roll it out to 1-cm (¹/₂-in)thick and cover with plastic wrap. Leave to rest for 15 minutes. Unwrap dough and cut into 2.5-cm (1-in) squares. Place dough squares 5 cm (2 in) apart on a lightly floured surface and leave to rest until dough is almost doubled in size.

Just before serving, heat oil in large pan or wok to 180°C (350°F). Fry 4–5 beignets at a time in hot oil for 3–4 minutes. Turn with wooden chopsticks or tongs to ensure beignets brown evenly. Drain on paper towels.

Prepare cinnamon sugar. Mix together ground cinnamon and sugar. Toss beignets in cinnamon sugar.

Serve oolong apple cider with beignets.

Basic Stocks

This handful of basic recipes, most of them stocks, form the foundation of every good kitchen, whether at home or in a restaurant. Throughout the world, the kitchens of The Peninsula Hotels use vegetable, fish, shellfish, chicken, veal and beef stock behind their sauces, gravies and soups. It is tempting, in this fast-as-digital age, to resort to commercial, instant dried or canned stocks, snatched off the supermarket shelf. Of course you are forgiven if you occasionally must. Yet if you take the time to make a stock from scratch, you are assured of the excellent quality of ingredients that go into the stock, which in turn improves the quality of your dish. Cooked slowly, with every flavour extracted from a natural ingredient, stocks become the foundation of your cooking.

Chicken Stock

Makes about 1 litre (32 fl oz / 4 cups)

Water *4 litres (32 fl oz / 4 cups)*

Chicken bones *2 kg (4 lb 6 oz), chopped and rinsed; soaked for 30 minutes*

Leek *100 g (3¹/₂ oz) use white part, peeled and cut into 2.5-cm (1-in) cubes*

Carrot *55 g (2 oz), peeled and cut into 2.5-cm (1-in) cubes*

Onion *55 g (2 oz), peeled and cut into 2.5-cm (1-in) cubes*

Celery *55 g (2 oz), cut into 2.5-cm (1-in) cubes*

Parsley *10 sprigs*

Thyme *5 stalks*

White peppercorns *1 Tbsp*

Bring water to a boil and blanch chicken bones for 2 minutes over high heat. Lower heat and skim off any scum from surface of stock. Add remaining ingredients and simmer over low heat for 1 hour.

Strain through a fine mesh sieve and return to the pot. Reduce to 1 litre (32 fl oz / 4 cups) over low heat. Leave to cool. Store refrigerated.

Veal Stock

Makes about 1 litre (32 fl oz / 4 cups)

Water *4 litres (128 fl oz / 16 cups)*

Veal bones *2 kg (4 lb 6 oz), chopped and rinsed for 30 minutes*

Leek *105 g (3¹/₂ oz), use white part, cut into 2.5-cm (1-in) cubes*

Carrot *55 g (2 oz), peeled and cut into 2.5-cm (1-in) cubes*

Onion *55 g (2 oz), peeled and cut into 2.5-cm (1-in) cubes*

Celery *55 g (2 oz), cut into 2.5-cm (1-in) cubes*

Parsley *10 sprigs*

Thyme *5 sprigs*

White peppercorns *1 Tbsp*

Bring water to a boil and blanch veal bones in water for 4 minutes over high heat. Lower heat and skim off any scum from surface of stock. Add remaining ingredients and simmer over low heat for 1 hour.

Strain through a fine mesh sieve and return to the pot. Reduce to 1 litre (32 fl oz / 4 cups) over low heat. Leave to cool. Store refrigerated.

Lamb Stock

Makes about 1 litre (32 fl oz / 4 cups)

Carrot *55 g (2 oz), peeled and cut into 2.5-cm (1-in) cubes*

Onion *45 g (1¹/₂ oz), peeled and cut into 2.5-cm (1-in) cubes*

Celery *45 g (1¹/₂ oz), cut into 2.5-cm (1-in) cubes*

Corn oil *2 Tbsp*

Garlic *3 cloves, peeled and left whole*

Tomato paste *55 g (2 oz)*

Canned peeled tomatoes *85 g (3 oz)*

Red wine *210 ml (7 fl oz)*

Rosemary *4 sprigs*

Thyme *4 sprigs*

Bay leaves *2*

Lamb bones *1 kg (2 lb 3 oz)*

Water *2 litres (64 fl oz / 8 cups)*

Port wine *105 ml (3¹/₂ fl oz)*

Cold butter *30 g (1 oz)*

Fine salt *¹/₄ tsp*

Ground black pepper *¹/₈ tsp*

In a stockpot, sauté carrot, onion, celery and garlic in corn oil until onion is translucent. Add tomato paste and canned peeled tomatoes. After 1 minute, deglaze with red wine and add rosemary, thyme and bay leaves.

Add bones and water and bring to a boil, then lower heat and simmer for about 2 hours. Skim off any froth that surfaces during the process.

Strain stock through a cloth-lined strainer, then reduce with port wine over low heat to about 1 litre (32 fl oz / 4 cups). Stir in cold butter, then season with salt and pepper.

Lobster Stock

Makes about 2 litres (64 fl oz / 8 cups)

Olive oil *60 ml (2 fl oz / 4 Tbsp)*

Live lobster *1.5 kg (3 lb 4¹/₂ oz), heads removed, bodies quartered*

Fennel *195 g (6¹/₂ oz), chopped*

Carrots *240 g (8¹/₂ oz), chopped*

Mushrooms *180 g (6¹/₂ oz), chopped*

Shallots *4*

Dry vermouth *240 ml (8 fl oz / 1 cup)*

Water *6 litres (192 fl oz / 24 cups)*

Garlic *4 cloves*

Tarragon *30 g (1 oz)*

Tomatoes *180 g (6¹/₂ oz), chopped*

Heat oil in a large pot over medium heat until oil smokes. Add lobster segments and sauté for 3–4 minutes until they turn red. Add fennel, carrots, mushrooms and shallots. Continue cooking for another 10 minutes.

Add vermouth, water, garlic, tarragon and tomatoes. Bring to a boil, then cover and simmer over low heat for 2–3 hours.

Strain stock through a conical sieve, pressing down and breaking shells and vegetables to extract as much stock as possible. Pour stock through a fine mesh strainer, tapping sides of strainer to release liquid. Leave to cool. Store refrigerated.

Fish Stock

Makes about 1 litre (32 fl oz / 4 cups)

Fish bones *500 g (1 lb 1¹/₂ oz), cleaned, chopped in small pieces and rinsed*

Onion *85 g (3 oz), peeled and sliced*

Celery *85 g (3 oz), sliced*

Leek *85 g (3 oz), sliced*

White peppercorns *1 Tbsp, crushed*

Bay leaf *1*

White wine *105 ml (3¹/₂ fl oz)*

Cold water *1.2 litres (40 fl oz / 5 cups)*

Place all ingredients into a stockpot and bring to a boil. When water comes to a boil, lower heat and simmer for 20 minutes. Skim off any scum from surface of stock.

Strain through a fine mesh sieve and return to the pot. Reduce to 1 litre (32 fl oz / 4 cups) over low heat. Leave to cool. Store refrigerated.

Vegetable Stock

Makes about 3 litres (96 fl oz / 12 cups)

White onions *300 g (11 oz), peeled and cut into 2.5-cm (1-in) cubes*

Carrots *300 g (11 oz), peeled and cut into 2.5-cm (1-in) cubes*

Leeks *300 g (11 oz), peeled and cut into 2.5-cm (1-in) cubes*

Celery *300 g (11 oz), cut into 2.5-cm (1-in) cubes*

Cabbage *300 g (11 oz)*

Lettuce *300 g (11 oz)*

Lemongrass *55 g (2 oz)*

Ginger *55 g (2 oz), peeled*

Chervil *55 g (2 oz)*

Water *4 litres (128 fl oz / 16 cups)*

Fine salt *20 g (²/₃ oz)*

Place all ingredients into a large stockpot and bring slowly to a boil. Lower heat and simmer for about 1 hour.

Strain through a cloth-lined strainer. Leave to cool. Store refrigerated.

How to steep tea:
When steeping tea, the temperature of the water is important to produce a cup of perfectly brewed tea. Always use filtered cold water and bring it to a boil. Use boiling water for black and pu'er teas, and water cooled to 75°–85°C (167°–185°F) for green and white teas. Unless specified in the recipe, you need only 1 tsp tea leaves for 250 ml (8 fl oz / 1 cup) of regular strength tea. When the water is at the correct temperature, add tea and leave to stand for the amount of time specified in the recipe. A general rule of thumb is 3–5 minutes for black tea, 1–9 minutes for oolong tea, 1–2 minutes for green tea and 4–15 minutes for white tea. Taste tea to check that it is to your liking. Strain out the leaves unless otherwise stated. Do not overcook tea as this will result in bitter-tasting tea.

How to make pasta:
Break eggs into flour mixture. Brewed tea and tea leaves may also be added at this stage. Stir in by hand, bringing dry ingredients into the mix until you have a loose ball of dough. Turn dough onto a floured work service and knead until smooth. Divide dough into several pieces, if necessary. Flatten dough slightly and put it through the pasta machine several times, adjusting it to a thinner setting each time. Whenever necessary, lightly sprinkle dough with flour to prevent sticking. When the sheet is thin enough, put the dough through the cutting blades and cut into strips of desired thickness.

How to make genmai cha soufflé: Prepare the soufflé moulds. Coat the inside of the moulds well with butter. Add ginger sugar and ground rice and turn moulds around to coat well. Pour off any remaining sugar and rice. Set moulds aside. Mix pastry cream with tea powder in a mixing bowl and set aside. Beat egg whites (preferably at room temperature) on high speed until frothy. Gradually add sugar and lemon juice and beat until medium peaks form. Spoon mixture into mixing bowl with pastry cream and tea powder. Fold mixture in lightly. Divide mixture into prepared moulds until about three-quarters full, then bake in a preheated oven immediately.

How to grind tea mixtures: Place tea leaves into a clean spice grinder or blender and grind until fine. Add any other ingredients as stated in the recipe, and grind again to achieve a fine powder.

How to shell a cooked lobster: Snap off the claws of the lobster and set aside. Dislodge the lobster head and set it aside, then place the back of the lobster tail in the palm of your hand. Squeeze hard until the shell cracks before pulling it apart to reveal the flesh underneath. Gently ease the tail flesh out and set aside; discard shell. Hold a claw in your hand and snap it in half at the joint. Take the smaller part and cut through the shell, but not the flesh, with a carving knife. Break open the shell at the cut and continue to cut the shell open with a pair of clean kitchen shears. When all of the shell is removed, extract the flesh and set aside. Run a sharp paring knife around the flesh of the claw before easing it out. Repeat the steps for the other claw.

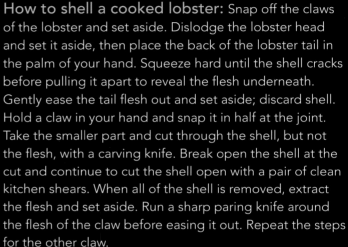

How to smoke an ingredient: Use a thick, deep cooking pan for this. A wok, Dutch oven or casserole is possible for this, and cast iron is ideal. To protect the pan, line it with aluminium foil. Heat the pan and sprinkle the smoking mixture as specified in the recipe into the pan. Place a cooking rack over, then place the ingredient to be smoked on the rack. Cover with a tight-fitting lid or a lid lined with aluminium foil to keep the smoke in the pan. Allow to smoke for the time stated in the recipe.

How to make custard-based ice cream:

Heat milk and cream, stirring constantly, until just about to boil. Any flavouring may be added to the mixture at this time. In a separate bowl, whisk egg yolks and sugar until well-mixed. Temper the egg yolk mixture by adding about one-third of hot milk and cream mixture ladle by ladle, stirring constantly. Pour tempered mixture into remaining milk and cream mixture, whisking constantly. Place over medium-low heat, stirring constantly with a whisk or wooden spoon to make custard. Custard is done as soon as a finger drawn across a wooden spoon leaves a track. Strain mixture to avoid lumps and allow to cool. Pour custard into an ice cream maker and churn according to the manufacturer's directions. Keep ice cream in the freezer until needed.

How to make froth or foam:

Prepare ingredients for foaming, then place into a blender and purée until fine. Strain puréed mixture by passing through a fine mesh sieve into a clean saucepan. Some recipes may not require straining. Stir in soy lecithin and season to taste as directed in the recipe. Use a hand-held blender, held at the surface of the liquid, to blend in butter or margarine a little at a time, or as directed in the recipe, until fully incorporated and sauce is foamy.

Chrysanthemum Tea

Chamomile Tea

Black Tea

White Tea

Lemongrass Tea

Tie Guan Yin

Peppermint Tea

Genmai Cha

Rose Hip Tea

Glossary

TEA AND HERBAL TISANES

Peppermint Tea is made from the dried leaves of the Mentha piperita, a perennial herb that is part of the large family of mints. Only the leaves are used in the preparation of this tea, which may also be brewed from the fresh peppermint leaves. Peppermint tea is popularly consumed to help calm the nerves, relieve headaches and ease digestive disorders.

Lemongrass Tea Lemongrass (*Cymbopogon citratus*) is a tall aromatic grass that releases a refreshing lemon-citrus fragrance when bruised. It is used both as a culinary and medicinal herb in Southeast Asia. The tea is made from dried lemongrass, and it is believed to treat fevers, coughs and colds; relieve flatulence, colic and stomach cramps; and aid digestion.

Genmai Cha This Japanese green tea is combined with roasted brown rice kernels, known as "*genmai*," some of which pop during roasting, so they look like tiny popcorn kernels. Genmai cha has a mild flavour and a nutty, roasted aroma.

Rose Hip Tea Rose hip is the fruit of the rose flower. It is shaped like a small apple and usually turns red as it matures. The mature rose hip is sliced and dried to make tea. Red-pink in colour, the infused rose hip tea has a distinctive tangy flavour, and is rich in vitamin C. It also contains vitamins A, D and E and is believed to help relieve headaches and dizziness.

Chrysanthemum Tea Made either from the dried flowers of *Chrysanthemum morifolium* or *Chrysanthemum indicum*, this caffeine-free floral tisane has a light colour and pleasant, sweet fragrance. This popular Chinese tea is believed to have "cooling" properties to lower body heat and relieve fevers and sore throats.

Chamomile Tea Usually made from the daisy-like flower of the German chamomile (*Matricaria recutita*) or Roman chamomile (*Chamaemelum nobile*), chamomile tea has a delicate floral fragrance with a calming effect. It is believed to promote sleep and help with a range of health ailments, including relieving colds and menstrual cramps.

Tie Guan Yin Literally translated as "iron goddess," tie guan yin is one of the most well-known and popular Chinese teas. It is a sub-variety of the semi-oxidized oolong tea, which is primarily produced in Fujian province in China and Taiwan. Tie guan yin tea leaves are tightly rolled and they produce a golden yellow infusion, with a sweet, floral fragrance.

White Tea In harvesting leaves for tea, the freshly picked young leaves of the *Camellia sinensis* plant are roasted shortly after harvest to dry out moisture in the leaves and retain their green characteristics. White tea consists only of the young top buds or top bud plus the next leaf, which are picked once a year in the spring. At this stage, the bud is still covered with fine white hairs (hence its name) and has not developed chlorophyll, the compound that turns foliage green. Thus the resulting tea leaves are pale and greyish-white in colour. White teas undergo little processing and are not fermented. They have a light, sweet flavour and are one of the most expensive types of teas.

Black Teas are fully oxidized, as opposed to oolong teas which are semi-oxidized, and green and white teas which are not oxidized at all. Some black teas, such as Lapsang Souchong, are roasted after full-oxidation with the smoke of the roasting process infusing the tea leaves. In Chinese, fully oxidized tea is known as "red tea" (*hong cha*). Black teas have a robust, full-bodied flavour.

Frisée

Chinese Mustard Green

Ginseng

Soy Lecithin

Togarashi Pepper

Couscous

Pink Peppercorns

Red Dates

Broad Beans

Celeriac

Yam Bean

Lemongrass

Fennel

GREENS, HERBS AND OTHERS

Broad Beans When choosing fresh broad beans in pods, select those where the beans are not bulging from the pods, as this indicates younger, more tender beans. The beans have very tough skin which can be removed by blanching briefly in boiling water.

Celeriac Root Also known as celery root, this versatile vegetable is the root of a special celery cultivated specifically for its root, and can be eaten raw or cooked. It ranges in size from a common apple to a small melon and has white flesh which tastes similar to a blend of celery and parsley. Choose firm and small to medium-size celeriac.

Couscous This pasta is made from coarsely ground durum wheat (semolina). It can be steamed or boiled like rice. Instant couscous takes just 10 minutes to cook while the traditional variety takes at least 2 hours. Couscous is a staple food in the Middle East and North Africa, where it is commonly served with meat or vegetable stews.

Fennel This vegetable consists of a broad bulbous base with short stalks and feathery leaves. Recipes calling for fennel usually use the bulb, which has a light and sweet aromatic flavour reminiscent of anise. Fennel can be eaten raw or cooked. Choose smaller bulbs as this means they are younger and less fibrous.

Frisée The spiky shape of its leaves makes frisée easily distinguishable from other salad greens. It holds its shape well and does not wilt easily. This firmness of texture and its mild bitter taste add contrast to salads, making frisée a popular salad green.

Chinese Mustard Green Also known as *gai choy*, the Cantonese name for several varieties of Chinese mustard greens, two varieties that are easily available commercially are the "big" and "small" mustard greens, but their use and taste are similar. Mustard greens are mainly cultivated for their thick, broad stems, which spot a distinctive ribbed pattern. The vegetable can be used raw, pickled or cooked. In texture, it is comparable to celery stems and in taste, it has a mild flavour with a touch of bitterness.

Ginseng This is the root-like rhizome of a wild plant in the genus panax that resembles ginger or turmeric root. It is an adaptogen, aphrodisiac and stimulant, and is often prescribed in traditional Chinese medicine and some contemporary energy drinks. In Chinese, it is known as "*renshen*" making reference to the fact that its common double root form resembles the legs of a human being. It is most often sold dry, whole or sliced.

Lemongrass This is a tall grass with a bulbous base and is widely used in Thai and Vietnamese cooking. When using, remove the hard outer leaves, trim the ends and use only the bulbous lower portion. Lemongrass has a refreshing and distinctive citrus flavour. The bulb should be bruised or pounded before cooking to fully release its flavour and aroma.

Pink Peppercorns This small, exotic, round dried fruit from Brazil is commonly mistaken to be part of the peppercorn family because of its name, but it is in fact the fruit of the Baies Rose. Pink peppercorns are sweet and peppery and are also available as part of a pepper blend from gourmet food stores.

Red Dates Also known as jujube or in Chinese as *hong zao*, red dates are the mature fruit of a small deciduous tree. Red dates play an important role in Traditional Chinese Medicine (TCM), as they are believed to enhance the functions of the stomach and spleen. These sweet, wrinkled dried fruit can as be enjoyed as a snack or boiled in soups and steeped in teas.

Soy Lecithin Used extensively in commercial food processing, soy lecithin was originally a by-product of soy bean oil. It is an emulsifier, holding fat and liquid together and preventing them from separating. Classified as a "phospholipid," it is today used by fine dining chefs to hold together liquids being whipped into froth or foam. It may be purchased at some natural food stores.

Togarashi Pepper This Japanese spice blend commonly comprises red chilli flakes, black pepper, seaweed, citrus and sesame seeds, although the mix may vary from brand to brand or from chef to chef. It is available at most Japanese supermarkets and some gourmet food stores.

Yam Bean (Jicama) A root vegetable belonging to the legume family (*Pachyrhizus erosus*), also known as Chinese turnip, Chinese potato, Mexican yam and Mexican potato. Common in the tropical Americas, it is also grown in tropical Asia. It is usually eaten peeled and raw. It has a sweet taste and crispy texture, comparable to fresh water chestnuts.

Weights and Measures

Quantities for this book are given in Metric and American (spoon and cup) measures. Standard spoon and cup measurements used are: 1 teaspoon = 5 ml, 1 tablespoon = 15 ml, 1 cup = 250 ml. All measures are level unless otherwise stated.

LIQUID AND VOLUME MEASURES

Metric	Imperial	American
5 ml	$^1/_6$ fl oz	1 teaspoon
10 ml	$^1/_3$ fl oz	1 dessertspoon
15 ml	$^1/_2$ fl oz	1 tablespoon
60 ml	2 fl oz	$^1/_4$ cup (4 tablespoons)
85 ml	$2^1/_2$ fl oz	$^1/_3$ cup
90 ml	3 fl oz	$^3/_8$ cup (6 tablespoons)
125 ml	4 fl oz	$^1/_2$ cup
180 ml	6 fl oz	$^3/_4$ cup
250 ml	8 fl oz	1 cup
300 ml	10 fl oz ($^1/_2$ pint)	$1^1/_4$ cups
375 ml	12 fl oz	$1^1/_2$ cups
435 ml	14 fl oz	$1^3/_4$ cups
500 ml	16 fl oz	2 cups
625 ml	20 fl oz (1 pint)	$2^1/_2$ cups
750 ml	24 fl oz ($1^1/_5$ pints)	3 cups
1 litre	32 fl oz ($1^3/_5$ pints)	4 cups
1.25 litres	40 fl oz (2 pints)	5 cups
1.5 litres	48 fl oz ($2^2/_5$ pints)	6 cups
2.5 litres	80 fl oz (4 pints)	10 cups

DRY MEASURES

Metric	Imperial
30 grams	1 ounce
45 grams	1½ ounces
55 grams	2 ounces
70 grams	2½ ounces
85 grams	3 ounces
100 grams	3½ ounces
110 grams	4 ounces
125 grams	4½ ounces
140 grams	5 ounces
280 grams	10 ounces
450 grams	16 ounces (1 pound)
500 grams	1 pound, 1½ ounces
700 grams	1½ pounds
800 grams	1¾ pounds
1 kilogram	2 pounds, 3 ounces
1.5 kilograms	3 pounds, 4½ ounces
2 kilograms	4 pounds, 6 ounces

OVEN TEMPERATURE

	°C	°F	Gas Regulo
Very slow	120	250	1
Slow	150	300	2
Moderately slow	160	325	3
Moderate	180	350	4
Moderately hot	190/200	370/400	5/6
Hot	210/220	410/440	6/7
Very hot	230	450	8
Super hot	250/290	475/550	9/10

LENGTH

Metric	Imperial
0.5 cm	¼ inch
1 cm	½ inch
1.5 cm	¾ inch
2.5 cm	1 inch

ABBREVIATION

tsp	teaspoon
Tbsp	tablespoon
g	gram
kg	kilogram
ml	millilitre

THE PENINSULA

HOTELS

The Peninsula Hong Kong

The Peninsula New York

The Peninsula Chicago

The Peninsula Beverly Hills

The Peninsula Bangkok

The Peninsula Beijing

The Peninsula Manila

The Peninsula Tokyo

The Peninsula Bangkok
333 Charoennakorn Road, Klongsan
Bangkok 10600, Thailand
Telephone: (66-2) 861 2888 Facsimile: (66-2) 861 1112
E-mail: pbk@peninsula.com

The Peninsula Beijing
8 Goldfish Lane, Wangfujing
Beijing 100006, People's Republic of China
Telephone: (86-10) 8516 2888 Facsimile: (86-10) 6510 6311
E-mail: pbj@peninsula.com

The Peninsula Beverly Hills
9882 South Santa Monica Boulevard
Beverly Hills, CA 90212, United States of America
Telephone: (1-310) 551 2888 Facsimile: (1-310) 788 2319
E-mail: pbh@peninsula.com

The Peninsula Chicago
108 East Superior Street (at North Michigan Avenue)
Chicago, IL 60611, United States of America
Telephone: (1-312) 337 2888 Facsimile: (1-312) 751 2888
E-mail: pch@peninsula.com

The Peninsula Hong Kong
Salisbury Road, Kowloon
Hong Kong, SAR, People's Republic of China
Telephone: (852) 2920 2888 Facsimile: (852) 2722 4170
E-mail: phk@peninsula.com

The Peninsula Manila
Corner of Ayala & Makati Avenues
1226 Makati City, Metro Manila, Philippines
Telephone: (63-2) 887 2888 Facsimile: (63-2) 815 4825
E-mail: pmn@peninsula.com

The Peninsula New York
700 Fifth Avenue at 55th Street
New York, NY 10019, United States of America
Telephone: (1-212) 956 2888 Facsimile: (1-212) 903 3949
E-mail: pny@peninsula.com

The Peninsula Shanghai (opening 2009)
No 32 The Bund, 32 Zhongshan Dong Yi Road
Shanghai 200002, People's Republic of China
E-mail: psh@peninsula.com

The Peninsula Tokyo
1-8-1 Yurakucho, Chiyoda-ku
Tokyo, 100-0006, Japan
Telephone: (81-3) 6270 2888 Facsimile: (81-3) 6270 2000
E-mail: ptk@peninsula.com

For more information, please visit us at www.peninsula.com

Project Coordination
Paul Tchen and Lisa Lum

Culinary Coordination
Oliver Dudler and Terrence Crandall

Project and Recipe Contributors
Dan Bark, Ian Barner, Sumalee Boon-eak, Patrice Cabannes, Wan Kwok Chung, Anthony Coriell, Terrence Crandall, Eric David, Holger Deh, Franco Diaz, Gerhard Doll, Anthony Darroman, Oliver Dudler, Uwe Faust, Miguel Franco, Tam Kwok Fung, Raymond Garcia, David Goodridge, Sean Hardy, Johnathan Kinsella, Paul Lau, William Lin, Jimmy MacMillan, Ed Madela, Alexander Y. Martinez, Adam Mathis, Michelle Medina, Joelle Moles, Anuwat Morakotjantachote, Bernhard G. Mueller, Stuart Newbigging, Shigeru Nojima, Thomas Piede, Garrison Price, Anthony Raymond, Maximilian von Reden, Nicole L. Sandlin, Noel Silva, Calvin Soh, Amy Sutton, Sherrie C. Tan, Florian Trento, Chan Wai, Ivan Yuen, Frank Ziegler

Photoshoot Location
The Peninsula Chicago

The Hongkong and Shanghai Hotels, Limited
8th Floor, St. George's Building, 2 Ice House Street, Central, Hong Kong
www.hshgroup.com

The Hon Sir Michael Kadoorie, Chairman
Ian D Boyce, Deputy Chairman
Clement K M Kwok, Managing Director and Chief Executive Officer
Mark Broadley, Finance Director and Chief Financial Officer
Peter C Borer, Director and Chief Operating Officer

Peninsula Merchandising Limited
5th Floor, The Peninsula Office Tower, 18 Middle Road, Tsim Sha Tsui, Kowloon, Hong Kong
www.peninsulaboutique.com

Paul Tchen, General Manager
Martin Yim, Manager – Operations and Business Development
Shelly Siu, Manager - Merchandise Development

Editor Lydia Leong
Design and Art Direction David Yip and Lynn Chin Nyuk Ling
Photography Edmond Ho, Jambu Studio
Text Olivia Wu
Recipe Testing Amanda Bowman and Nick Cobarrusvias
Nutrition Advisor Gabrielle K. Tuscher
Special Thanks Rodrick J. Markus, Rare Tea Cellar

Copyright © 2007 Peninsula Merchandising Limited
A subsidiary of The Hongkong and Shanghai Hotels, Limited

Published by Marshall Cavendish Cuisine
An imprint of Marshall Cavendish International
1 New Industrial Road, Singapore 536196

Marshall Cavendish is a trademark of Times Publishing Limited

National Library Board Singapore Cataloguing in Publication Data

Naturally Peninsula, tea flavours / [editor, Lydia Leong ; photography, Edmond Ho ; text, Olivia Wu]. – Singapore : Marshall Cavendish Cuisine, c2007.
p. cm.

ISBN-13 : 978-981-261-514-5
ISBN-10 : 981-261-514-8

1. Cookery (Tea) I. Leong, Lydia. II. Ho, Edmond, 1967-
III. Wu, Olivia.

TX817.T3
641.6372 -- dc22   OCN166728777

Printed by Times International Printing

Naturally Peninsula
"To live well is to eat well"